THE MAN'S

GROOMING
SURVIVAL GUIDE

**LOOKING YOUR BEST
AT HOME AND ON THE GO**

**THE EDITORS OF SHARPMAN.COM®
FIRST EDITION**

**SHARPMAN PRESS
LOS ANGELES, CALIFORNIA**

THE SHARPMAN'S GROOMING SURVIVAL GUIDE:
LOOKING YOUR BEST AT HOME AND ON THE GO

by The Editors of SharpMan.com®

PUBLISHED BY:
SharpMan Press
11718 Barrington Court
No. 702
Los Angeles, CA 90049 U.S.A.
orders@sharpman.com
http://www.sharpman.com

For information about permission to reproduce selections from this book, write to Permissions, SharpMan Press, 11718 Barrington Court, No. 702, Los Angeles, CA 90049-2930 or permissions@sharpman.com.

The trademark SharpMan.com® is registered with the U.S. Patent and Trademark Office.

ISBN: 0-9706600-2-2

Library of Congress Control Number: 2001096984

Printed in the United States of America

Art direction by Rowan Moore for Designland

10   9   8   7   6   5   4   3   2   1

TABLE OF CONTENTS

Got a grooming question? Simply look it up in the table of contents or index of this guidebook.

That's it.

No need to read the book from cover to cover.
This guidebook is designed for use by busy guys on an as-needed basis. The answers to SharpMen's most common grooming questions are organized one after the other, as follows:

> **THE GROOMING ISSUE:**
> *The name of the grooming topic.*
>
> **THE FACTS:**
> *A brief explanation of why the grooming issue arises.*
>
> **THE GROOMING SOLUTION:**
> *Straightforward tips to meet your specific grooming need, often in a step-by-step format.*
>
> **REQUIRED GEAR:**
> *A listing of the tools required to accomplish your grooming goal.*

And you're done.

Looking sharp isn't about great genetics or daily workouts. Humphrey Bogart probably couldn't have benched 300 and would have starved as an underwear model, but the ladies loved him.

Looking sharp is about *maximizing* on your physical attributes. For example, your hair type and the shape of your face can help determine your best cut or facial hair option. *The SharpMan's Grooming Survival Guide* will help you capitalize on *what you've got.*

Looking sharp also means not losing on the *easy* points. Women, employers and clients alike are turned off by ingrown toenails, overpowering cologne and poor posture. *The SharpMan's Grooming Survival Guide* will clue you in to common grooming missteps.

And don't bother reading from cover to cover. This guidebook is designed to be a handy reference for use on an as-needed basis. Simply scan the table of contents or the index to find the answer to your immediate grooming question. You'll get step-by-step tips on how to sharpen your look *fast.* We've even thrown in a list of required gear for your next trip to the store. *That's it.*

SHARP FACIAL HAIR

SHARPSKIN

EAR CARE

SHARPMOUTH

THE GROOMING ISSUE: THE SHARP SHAVE

THE FACTS:

It's Monday morning, and that swarthy look that took the better part of the weekend to achieve has got to go. A few simple tips can make the difference between a great shave and a face covered with toilet tissue.

THE GROOMING SOLUTION:

Step One: Open your pores. Cheer up! You plan to bathe, don't you? If so, you'll be taking the first step to a great shave. Go ahead and turn on the shower. A good shave requires heat to open up your pores and allow the blade's edge to do the job it was designed to do.

That's right, gentlemen, we said *blade,* so throw that new electric razor in the drawer. No electric, whether black, chrome, digital or waterproof can beat a blade. Just ask your father. Chances are he never

REQUIRED GEAR

• Twin-or triple-blade razor.
• Shaving cream.

used that fancy shaving gadget you bought him last Father's Day. If he says otherwise, he's either lying or too old to remember the perks that come with a close shave.

Step Two: Prepare your tools. Complete your shower, allowing the steam to linger in your bathroom. Turn on the hot water - and only the hot water - in your sink and drop in your blade. Remember, *heat is your friend.* After a few minutes, add only as much cool water as you need to avoid a visit to the local burn center, and wet your face thoroughly.

Step Three: Apply your shaving cream. That's shaving *cream.* Not foam. Not gel. If the contents are under pressure, for a few dollars more, you can do better. But whatever product you choose, be careful to apply it to only those areas that you intend to shave. The outline you create will be your guide, and when all is gone, you'll know you're done.

Step Four: Pick up your blade and start with the side opposite to your dominant hand. In other words, if you are right-handed, start with the left side of your face. This is the easiest part of your shave and, given the fact that your eyes are still half-glued shut from attending your buddy's Sunday Night Tequilafest, you'll be less likely to scar yourself. Most men fear blades because few enjoy seeing their own blood in the morning. To avoid this, use long, smooth, consistent strokes over your face, with just enough pressure to prevent the blade from snagging, but not so much that you gouge your skin.

Your strokes should run the blade down your cheek. That's *down,* not up, and not sideways. It's remarkable how many men still believe that a close shave requires going "against the grain." Shaving is like painting a wood fence: go with the grain, always. Any other way, and you run the risk of irritating your skin.

If you aren't satisfied with the closeness of your shave, simply change blades. Most twin—or triple-blade razors will do the job for five to ten days, depending on the strength of your beard. If your shave is not as close as you would like, or your current blade begins to feel rough against your skin, then it's time to discard the blade and pick up a new one.

Step Five: Rinse. Place your blade back under the warm water after every three strokes, and, when finished, rinse your face thoroughly. This last step is important, not only for the obvious goal of removing lingering cream, but because it's a fast way to check your work. If you feel any missed stubble as you rinse, just pick up your blade and touch up.

Step Six: Gently pat your face dry. Don't rub. If you use cologne or aftershave, apply it first to your body; whatever is still left on your hands is more than enough for your freshly shaven skin.

THE GROOMING ISSUE: Avoiding Razor Burn

THE FACTS:

For some, shaving is like going into battle. If you prepare, your chances of coming out without a burn are greatly enhanced. On the other hand, if you jump into battle with no protection, your skin will suffer the fiery consequences.

REQUIRED GEAR

- Shaving cream.
- Twin- or triple-blade razor.
- Moisturizing aftershave.
- Tweezers.

THE GROOMING SOLUTION:

Although it sounds tedious, protecting your skin from the shaving battleground is easier than you think. Dermatologists recommend a simple regimen of preparing the skin, choosing super-sensitive tools, and following up with a moisturizing aftershave. Even in extreme cases, simple over-the-counter products can heal the most severe razor burn.

Step One: Prepare for the fight. Most guys assume that avoiding razor burn requires the exclusive use of an electric razor – and the chance of missing out on a close shave. Not so. Simply showering before you shave will properly prepare your hair follicles and pores for a razor-burn-free shave and minimize existing irritation. For more information, see *The Sharp Shave* section of this guidebook.

Step Two: Choose a moisturizing shaving cream for your morning ritual. The more emollient your shaving product, the less likely you will be to develop dry-skin related irritation. As you shave, don't skimp on the shaving cream; to avoid razor burn, make sure your entire shaving area is lathered. Then, when shaving, angle your razor *with* the grain, pointed down, to prevent causing further irritation or ingrown hairs. Don't press the razor too firmly on your skin. Gentle pressure is enough. Take your time and pay attention to the task at hand.

Step Three: Soothe your skin. After you've finished shaving, take a moment to be good to it. Splashing warm water on freshly shaven skin will close your pores and help prevent irritation. Following up with a moisturizing aftershave balm will do much more. Moisturizing aftershaves disinfect and add a bit more moisture to protect sensitive skin – particularly in those dry winter months when skin becomes more sensitive to shaving.

Step Four: Treat the wounds. If all the prep work in the world won't protect your skin from razor burn, moisturizing aftershave treatments containing *tea tree extract,* a natural ingredient that calms burns and prevents the build-up of irritating dead skin cells and ingrown hairs, are your best defense. Simply apply a small amount after you rinse off your shaving cream.

Got lots of ingrown hairs? Before using any aftershave product, remove more deeply embedded hairs with a pair of clean tweezers. To prevent tweezer pain, numb the area with an ice cube or over-the-counter numbing agent before hair removal.

SHARPNOTE: When buying a shaving aid, be sure to grab a *cream,* not a gel. Creams provide more moisture and offer better razor burn protection.

THE GROOMING ISSUE: FACIAL HAIR OPTIONS

THE FACTS:

Facial hair is associated with strong grooming statements and relaxed confidence. Better still, experimenting with facial hair can give you and your skin a short break from the daily shave routine–a plus for guys with sensitive skin.

THE GROOMING SOLUTION:

Before you make the move to the hairy side, consider your various facial hair options:

Mustache. That tuft of hair above the upper lip has many variations, is relatively easy to grow and requires very little maintenance. For today's trend and business climates, a neat, short mustache is best received.

Sideburns. Sideburns are easy to grow and maintain. Despite the recent upsurge in popularity for long, thick sideburns, your ideal length and width depends largely on the shape of your face and what your workplace will tolerate.

Full beard. The full beard covers the chin, jaw line and upper lip. Beards are easy to grow and ideal for masking scars and other skin or structural imperfections. Beards generally require a strong, full growth, but longer beard styles can cover patchy or uneven growth. Of course, having half of your face covered in hair is a pretty strong statement. Experimenting with this style will let you know if you can carry it off.

Goatee. The various goatee styles are all kid-brother versions of the full beard. They cover the chin area, but do not extend down beyond the jaw line. Because less facial hair area is required, goatees are relatively easy to grow and are ideal for men with patchy growth. Of course, all this comes at a price; consistent shaving and trimming are required to maintain that distinctive look. Goatees can be worn with or without a matching mustache. Mini-goatees, also known as "jazz dots," are also popular.

Combo styles. The combinations of mustaches, goatees and side-burns are unlimited and can be flattering. Of course, the more complicated your chosen design, the more shaving and trimming maintenance work it will require.

SHARPNOTE: Recognize that — however small — all facial hair styles make a statement. Men with more conservative professional lives may want to steer away from the more "hip" facial hair styles, such as goatees and jazz dots, due to concerns about appearing less serious. On the other hand, men whose livelihoods depend on looking *avant garde* may *require* them. Work-related travel schedules are another consideration. The less time you have for personal grooming, the less likely you are to commit to a high-maintenance style. Additionally, while working or traveling abroad, the presence or absence of facial hair may be viewed as unprofes-sional or untrustworthy.

See the *Choosing Facial Hair to Flatter the Shape of Your Face* section of this guidebook for more information.

THE GROOMING ISSUE: Choosing Facial Hair to Flatter the Shape of Your Face

THE FACTS:

Looking sharp is all about maximizing on what you have. Simply taking the shape of your face and other features into consideration before choosing a facial hair style can cut out a lot of your guess-work and yield great results.

THE GROOMING SOLUTION:

Match the general shape of your face and facial features to one of the following:

Long, thin face. SharpMen with long, thin faces look great when they fill out the look of their faces. If you're one of those, avoid longer beards and goatees, as they will add to the length to your chin. Instead, try a short pair of sideburns to round out your jaw line or a wide mustache. Both of these styles will draw attention away from the lower half of your face. For those who like full beards, keep them trimmed very tightly around the chin and leave the sides fuller.

Round, full face. Men with round faces can look "pudgy," even if their bodies are not. Often lengthening the look of your face can help. Try a goatee – goatees draw the eye to a point at the chin and make jaws look less full. Avoid narrow mustaches and any hair on the jaw line — these styles only add to the roundness of your face.

Small chin. SharpMen with small chins – also called "weak chins" – look great when they beef up this area of the face. A fuller goatee or beard can do wonders for drawing out your chin. Avoid mustaches without beards, as they will tend to overshadow your chin and bring you back to square one.

Square jaw. Feeling a bit robotic? While square jaws are traditionally associated with Romeos of the silver screen, there is such a thing as *too* much of a good thing. Try growing a rounded beard to soften your mug. If you plan to add sideburns, keep them narrow.

Thinning or no hair. Ever see guys with very little hair on their heads and *tons* of facial hair? Not a great look. Instead of fooling the eye, this combo creates an unbalanced look. SharpMen with little or no hair on their heads should compliment their look with only subtle facial hair features. A minimal beard or goatee, trimmed very tightly, looks great. Avoid fuller beard styles and sideburns.

Covering scarring. Facial hair is an excellent way to cover scars, but keep in mind that your hair cover should nonetheless suit the shape of your face. Even for guys with substantial acne scarring, a tightly trimmed beard or goatee can work just as well as the full job. For best results, grow the full beard first, mark the area you'd like to mask and style accordingly.

THE GROOMING ISSUE: GROWING FACIAL HAIR 101

THE FACTS:

Once you've decided to grow facial hair, simply following a few easy steps will ensure that you are able quickly determine which look is most flattering to you, with minimal re-growth time.

THE GROOMING SOLUTION:

Step One: Timing is everything. If possible, begin your experiment while on vacation. This way, if you feel self-conscious or would like to alter your new look, you'll be out of sight from friends and work colleagues during the transition. Another good reason to grow facial hair while away? Those first few weeks can look pretty unkempt – much more suited to time at the beach than a day at the office.

Step Two: Do nothing. Stop shaving and leave your face alone for about three weeks. Sounds simple, doesn't it? It's not. There's always a temptation to start trimming and shaping as soon as your hair gets past the stubble stage. Fight the urge. Trimming and shaping too early can result in removing too much hair in some places. The result? A longer wait, a style unsuited to your face, or frustration resulting in an early end to the experiment.

> ## REQUIRED GEAR
>
> • Twin- or triple-blade razor.
> • Electric beard trimmer.
> • Beard trimming scissors and comb.
> • Moisturizing aftershave with *tea tree extract.*

Step Three: Choose a shape. Once you have enough hair to work with, you can begin shaping your facial hair. If you are uncertain about what you want, make a list of all of the styles you like, beginning with the styles that require the most amount of hair (i.e., a full beard) and ending with those that require the least (i.e., a "jazz dot"). Begin experimenting with the styles at the beginning of your list. Give yourself a few days to test out each look before moving on to the next one. This way you'll have the opportunity to try out several different styles with a minimum of re-growth time in between. After all, it is easier to shave off hair than to grow back a gap you didn't want.

Step Four: Get professional help. Once you've chosen your basic style, visiting an old-fashioned men's barber shop may help you refine the look. Once your barber has set the "lines" of your new look, maintenance is as easy as following this outline.

Otherwise, get yourself a good pair of beard-trimming scissors and a comb. Use a twin- or triple-blade razor to define your look and use the comb and scissors to trim your hair to the desired length. Take your time and trim gradually until you hit upon the style you want. Alternatively, save time by investing in an inexpensive electric beard trimmer with various length settings.

SHARPNOTE: Itching is a common problem in the first few weeks of facial hair growth. To minimize itching, wash your face thoroughly and use a light moisturizer. Moisturizing aftershaves containing a natural ingredient called tea tree extract do double-duty: they moisturize and prevent the development of ingrown hairs.

See the *Facial Hair Maintenance* section of this guidebook for specific information on trimming and shaping.

THE GROOMING ISSUE: FACIAL HAIR MAINTENANCE

THE FACTS:

If you've gone to the trouble of growing out your facial hair, picking up a couple of trimming and maintenance tricks can go a long way towards ensuring your facial hair always looks sharp.

THE GROOMING SOLUTION:

Ideal maintenance. Once you've chosen your facial hair style and established the basic maintenance "lines," always trim and groom *outside* of those lines.

Keeping clean. To keep facial hair clean, use the same shampoo you use for the hair on your head and rinse thoroughly. For full beards or men with dry skin or course facial hair, using a small amount of hair conditioner will keep skin from flaking and tough facial hair from scarring the ladies.

REQUIRED GEAR

• Electric beard trimmer.
• A wide-toothed or narrow-toothed comb.
• A small pair of sharp scissors.

Using a beard trimmer. While it is possible to use scissors and a comb, an inexpensive electric beard trimmer will prove to be your best facial hair maintenance equipment. The various trimmer settings will help you quickly maintain and even out facial hair length (read: no bald spots), in addition to helping you define and maintain a clean neckline.

Combing out. Once you've cleaned and trimmed your facial hair, take a moment to quickly comb it into place. A wide-toothed comb works best on beards, while the narrow-toothed variety is ideal for mustaches, goatees and sideburns. Why not use your hairbrush? A comb has the added advantage of allowing you to easily isolate and trim unwanted hair as you go.

Trimming tips for beards. Beards look best when kept tight and well trimmed. To avoid a sloppy look, shave any hair below your jaw line every two or three days, depending on how aggressive your growth is. You can make this job easier by using an electric beard trimmer. The upper line of a beard is generally not shaved, unless you feel that the natural line of your beard is too high.

Trimming tips for mustaches. Keep your mustache trimmed above your upper lip to avoid being one of those guys who constantly has food caught in his facial hair. When trimming your mustache, begin by trimming from the middle and work your way out to each side.

Trimming tips for goatees. Goatee styles come and go. Fad is less important than finding a style that suits the shape of your face and maintaining it properly. In most cases, simply keeping your goatee short, clean and neat goes a long way. Shave around the ideal shape of the goatee, always on the *outside* of the line, and follow up with a quick scissor trim or an electric beard trimmer to maintain the length.

Trimming tips for other styles. Nearly all facial hair styles require you to shave and trim to avoid looking sloppy. Depending on your chosen style, you may prefer to use a beard trimmer to maintain the length of the hair and a razor for areas that require a clean shave.

THE GROOMING ISSUE: TRAINING FACIAL HAIR

THE FACTS:

For years SharpMen have "trained" their facial hair into totally unnatural — but then-fashionable — growth patterns. Think of the handlebar mustache or other gravity-defying facial hair styles. You think those hairs weren't coaxed?

Historically men have used mustache wax or paste, a small mustache comb and their fingers to coax facial hair into the desired style. Today's SharpMen can apply this technique to facial hair that grows at odd angles.

THE GROOMING SOLUTION:

Training products. To train your facial hair, choose a can of mustache wax or one of the many pomades, head hair waxes and gels currently on the market. The key is to find a product strong enough to hold your hair, but one that does not irritate your skin.

> ### REQUIRED GEAR
>
> • Pomade, gel or wax.
> • Narrow-toothed mustache comb.

SharpMen with oily skin may prefer a super-hold gel to avoid blemishes, while dry-haired SharpMen may wish to use a pomade to prevent flaking. When in doubt, ask your barber or hairstylist for a recommendation.

Training techniques. Once you've chosen your product, simply apply a small amount to your palm and then a smaller amount to your facial hair. Use less than you think you need – adding is a lot easier than washing out and starting over. Once you've applied your gel, pomade or wax, use a narrow-toothed comb to shape your hair, using the hair product as the "adhesive." Keep this up and your hair should eventually give in.

THE GROOMING ISSUE:
GROWING FULLER FACIAL HAIR

THE FACTS:

Some beards don't grow in evenly, making it difficult to grow a full beard, mustache or sideburns. Why is this?

Facial and body hair growth is controlled by the male hormone *testosterone* and any other hormones the body that converts into testosterone. Some men naturally produce less testosterone, which results in less body hair and patchy facial hair growth.

Is it possible to promote facial and body hair growth in the same way men block the thinning of head hair? Note really.

The amount of hair men retain on their heads is controlled by the amount of testosterone their bodies convert to *dihydrotestosterone* (DHT). SharpMen who tend to lose hair on their heads have a higher quantity of the enzyme responsible for this conversion. The most common hair loss suppressers – and the herb *Saw Palmetto* – block the activity of this conversion enzyme. Because of this, the application of head-hair treatments cannot help men grow fuller facial hair. Facial and body hair growth requires testosterone.

THE GROOMING SOLUTION:

To increase your amount of facial and body hair growth, speak to your doctor about taking testosterone supplements, available by prescription in a *transdermal* patch, injection, pill or gel form.

SHARPNOTE: Realize that taking testosterone supplements is a tricky business: some men's bodies have a tendency to more readily convert testosterone into DHT or even *estrogen*, the female hormone. For these men, taking testosterone supplements without proper supervision can cause them to lose their head hair or even increase their "breast" size!

THE GROOMING ISSUE:
DEALING WITH EAR & NOSE HAIR

THE FACTS:

Ever wake up one morning and discover a stray hair making its way out of your ear or nostril?   Beware the tentacles of terror – they look sloppy and unkempt.

REQUIRED GEAR

• Small blunt-nosed scissors, *or*
• Electric ear and nose hair trimmer.

SharpMen don't just *suddenly* sprout nose hair — it's always been there. Tiny ear and nose hairs act as barriers that protect the body from airborne dirt and pollen, the same way lashes protect the eye. As SharpMen get older, changing hormonal levels affect hair growth. The male hormone *dihydrotestosterone* (DHT), the culprit behind male pattern baldness, may also be linked to nasal and ear hair growth. This explains why women don't commonly experience similar problems. Although researchers have established that increased levels of DHT are responsible for scalp hair loss, the exact relationship of DHT to nasal and ear hair is unclear.

THE GROOMING SOLUTION:

Ever heard that trimming ear or nose hair causes it to grow back thicker? It's not true. Trimming unwanted hair does not cause more hair to grow. So feel free to trim any hair that doesn't suit your sense of style. But when we say trim, we mean *trim. Do not pluck.* Not only does plucking hurt, it may cause a tearing of the skin on the inside your nose, which can lead to infection.

To trim nose and ear hair, use a small pair of blunt-nosed scissors to carefully shorten your hairs. It is not necessary to trim too closely. Simply cut down those hairs that protrude from your nose and ears.

Alternatively, use an ear and nose hair trimmer, a small electric or battery-operated device that uses a rotating or oscillating blade to quickly and safely trim hair. Both mechanisms work well, although the oscillating blade is often considered less painful.

SHARPNOTE: Trimmers are safe to use, so long as you refrain from forcing them too far into your nasal cavity or ear canal. Always review the instructions before going where no man has gone before.

THE GROOMING ISSUE: TAMING THE "UNIBROW"

THE FACTS:

Having one long eyebrow span the area over both eyes makes some SharpMen uncomfortable. Why? In general, contemporary men's grooming ideals dictate that connected eyebrows look less polished than two distinct eyebrow lines.

THE GROOMING SOLUTION:

SharpMen have several options for removing the unwanted hair in between their eyebrows. The method you choose will largely depend on the strength of your growth, your budget and your willingness to maintain your eyebrows on a regular basis.

> ### REQUIRED GEAR
>
> • Slant-nosed metal tweezers.
> • Pencil or straight edge.
> • Alcohol or other antiseptic.
> • Cotton balls.

Tweezing. While hardly pleasurable, using a pair of slant-nosed metal tweezers to pluck the hair in between your eyebrows is often your easiest and least expensive option. You can tweeze in the privacy of your own home and remove stray hairs as they reappear. See below for step-by-step tips on safely plucking your unibrow.

Alternatively, consider visiting a professional for the initial grunt work. He or she will shape your brows and instruct you on maintaining your new look. Most aestheticians (professionals once known as "beauticians") who service women also accept male clients.

Waxing. Wax treatments involve spreading hot or cold wax over the area targeted for hair removal, placing a strip of cloth over the wax, rubbing vigorously and then ripping the cloth — along with the wax and the hair — in one smooth stroke. Waxing removes the hair and hair root, and is generally considered to be longer lasting than plucking, because your roots take several weeks to reestablish themselves. While more painful than plucking, waxing takes only seconds and the sting disappears quickly.

Although there are many home waxing kits that allow SharpMen to wax their own unibrows, consider going to a professional salon for this treatment. First-time home waxers have been known to injure themselves or wax off more hair than intended.

As with plucking, most aestheticians who service women also accept male clients.

Electrolysis. Electrolysis hair removal treatments use a small needle to pass electric currents to the root of the hair, thereby killing the root and permanently arresting the regrowth of your unibrow. Regardless of what you've seen on late-night infomercials, you'll need to go to a dermatologist or professional salon for this treatment. Since each hair is treated individually, full effect generally requires several sessions.

Laser. Laser hair removal treatments are relatively new and vary in technique. All claim to be permanent. The success and amount of treatment you require depend on the strength of your hair growth, the fullness of your unibrow and the color of your hair. The darker your hair, the more effective the treatment. SharpMen with very light eyebrows may not be able to utilize laser treatments at all.

One laser method uses pulsed light to remove hair and impair regrowth. A cool gel and a hand-held treatment unit are applied to the skin, followed by pulses of light that penetrate the skin and disable the hair follicles. When the gel is removed, much of the hair is wiped off with it. The remaining hair falls out within a week. Another treatment method passes a beam of light through the skin to the hair follicle, burning the hair but not your skin – *usually*. Each type of laser treatment session generally lasts twenty to sixty minutes.

Does any of this hurt? In some cases, a lot. With some laser light treatments, the closer the technician is to the bone, the more pain the patient feels. Then of course, there's the *burning*. Some laser hair removal lightly burns the skin surface in addition to the hair roots (and will leave a scab). Ever had a "light" burn? It hurts a bit, right? You can expect a similar discomfort from laser treatments. Of course, when compared to the short treatment time and permanence, many SharpMen may find that laser treatments are their best bet. Most laser treatment courses are slightly more expensive than electrolysis.

Maintenance. Even if you regularly visit a professional salon to have your unibrow cured, you will always need to do some home maintenance for stray hairs. Similarly, if your unibrow is not full enough to require a trip to the salon, consider the following tips for grooming and shaping your eyebrows:

Pluck just out of the shower. It is easier and less painful to tweeze hairs when you first get out of the shower, as the heat and steam will have opened your pores and loosened their grip on the hairs.

Map out your route. Where should each eyebrow begin and end? Hold a pencil or other straight edge against the end of your nose, straight up to your eyebrow. Your inner brow should begin where the pencil meets your brow and end about a quarter of an inch past the outer corner of your eye.

Removing hair. Grasping the tweezers with your thumb and forefinger, firmly grab and pluck away from your face using a single forceful movement. Only attempt to pluck one hair at a time to minimize pain. Refrain from picking at hairs too short for easy plucking to avoid breaking the skin.

Stop to assess. As you pluck, try to keep your work balanced. The last thing you want is for one eyebrow to be thinner or shorter than the other. For this reason, alternate plucking each brow every few hairs and watch the balance between the two.

Don't over-pluck. Pluck slowly and take away only those stray hairs that are particularly obvious. When in doubt, stop plucking. No SharpMan wants to be the guy with eyebrows that are too "done."

Clean up. When you've finished tweezing, wipe the area with an alcohol-soaked cotton ball to clean and close your pores.

SHARPNOTE: If you've spent money on a professional, let him or her determine the "line" of your eyebrows, and then only pluck *outside* of this line.

THE GROOMING ISSUE: WASHING UP 101

THE FACTS:

As you move from your teens to your twenties, from your twenties to your thirties, etc., your skin goes through frequent and extreme changes. With every year and every season, your skin experiences changes that require different types of care.

For some high-paced SharpMen, these changes

REQUIRED GEAR

• Non-drying soap or facial cleanser.
• Light exfoliant.
• Light moisturizer.
• Sunscreen with SPF 15 or greater.

occur even more often due to sudden climate changes involved in business travel, air travel, increased stress, heat or air conditioning, and changes in diet and exercise. Failing to change your skin care routine as your skin needs change may result in having your skin look less sharp than it could.

THE GROOMING SOLUTION:

Skin problems, types and products may vary, but the basics remain constant. The ideal skin care program includes four steps: cleansing, exfoliating, moisturizing and sun protection.

Sounds time consuming? It's not. You'll find that once you get into the habit of going through these steps, you'll easily cut your prep time to three minutes twice a day.

Step One: Clean. Before you do anything, always ensure that your skin is clean. While most guys grab the nearest bar of freebie hotel soap, consider picking up a bar or cleanser that promises not to over-dry — the gentler, the better, even if you don't have "sensitive skin."

Step Two: Scrub. Once your skin is clean, consider removing the patches of dead skin cells that naturally build up on the surface of your face. Doing so will help prevent blackheads and other break-outs. It is only necessary to use an exfoliant once or twice a week.

Step Three: Lube. Think you don't need to moisturize? Think again. A failure to utilize this simple tool often leads SharpMen to develop itchy beard growth, blotchy skin and breakouts. Guys who drink a lot of coffee, smoke cigarettes, work long hours in offices with windows that don't open or frequently travel by air need to lube up more than most.

Choose a moisturizer that is super light and "hypo-allergenic." Light products won't overwhelm your pores and cause breakouts. Does your skin have oily spots? Apply the moisturizer *around* these areas.

Moisturizing products work best when applied while your skin is still slightly damp from the shower. This helps lock in hydration.

Step Four: Screen. Sunscreen is your last and most important step. Yes, that means you. Even guys who only see the sun during a short morning commute require sun protection. A good sunscreen can make the difference between sharp-looking skin and skin that looks haggard and tired. Oh, yeah, and then there's that whole no-skin-cancer thing. A nice perk to great-looking skin.

Step Five: Pay attention to changes in your skin, and adjust accordingly. If you begin to peel in the winter months, cut down on the exfoliation and up your moisturizer; if you find your skin becoming oilier in the summer months, switch to a less drying soap, exfoliate more often and go light on the moisturizer. Depending on your workload and schedule, recognize that your skin is likely to change more often than the seasons, so stay on top of it.

SHARPNOTE: If you'd like to cut out a skin care step, look for a light moisturizer and sunscreen combo. Because sunscreen only lasts about an hour after application, go for the good stuff, SPF 15 or higher, to get the most for your money. Use a sunscreen-free moisturizer after your evening wash-up.

THE GROOMING ISSUE: ACNE

THE FACTS:

Most acne occurs in the form of whiteheads *(pustules),* blackheads, or more rarely, inflamed *papules* ("zits"). These papules are whiteheads plus bacteria.

The differences between these miseries are miniscule, but important. Normal pores produce oil, which functions as the skin's natural hydrator. When a pore becomes blocked, the oil builds up inside the pore, causing swelling and sometimes infection. Unclogging the pores is not as easy as it sounds. This is because our biggest ally — natural exfoliation — is also our biggest enemy.

REQUIRED GEAR

• Exfoliant.
• Matches.
• Needle.
• Cotton ball.
• Alcohol.
• Tissue paper.
• Facial mud.
• Light moisturizer.

Huh? Read on:

Your skin completely sheds itself and builds up anew every month or so. The problem is that skin sheds unevenly, leaving some new skin and other areas of dry and flaky old skin. So, while a whitehead is simply a pore blocked with your body's own hydration system, a blackhead is a whitehead that is topped off with a plug of dead skin and dirt.

These blackheads take weeks to form, so it makes sense that they don't disappear overnight. When bacteria find their way into a clogged pore, the pore becomes inflamed — red and irritated. Your body's natural defenses take over, and white blood cells flock to the area to attack the bacteria and blockage, creating a full-blown papule, or "zit."

THE GROOMING SOLUTION:

Most acne can be reduced or eliminated by simply washing your skin after your workouts and before you turn in at night. See the *Washing Up 101* section of this guidebook for more information.

Try scrubbing. Another option for arresting the development of acne is to add a manual exfoliant to your skin care regimen. Several "scrubs" are available on the market, but beware: many of the natural scrubs contain walnut shells and other rough ingredients that can tear your pores, causing scarring and even infection. Opt for manufactured scrubs that contain smooth beads that will not damage your skin; chemical scrubs, such as those containing *alpha hydroxy acid* ("AHA") or products that utilize your own rubbing action to remove dead skin cells.

Don't touch. In general, avoid picking at your face. Picking irritates existing acne and creates new acne by spreading bacteria.

Drain properly. If you've got a whitehead and a big week ahead of you, resist the urge to squeeze. "Popping" your blemishes causes the skin to burst unevenly, often creating bruising and an unsightly red scab.

Instead, take a quick shower to open your pores. Sterilize a small needle by holding it over a flame and gently puncture the top of the whitehead. Wrap a small piece of tissue paper around each of your forefingers and – using as little force as possible – help the puss gently ooze out of the escape valve you've created. The less you push, the less red and noticeable your former blemish will be.

Once the initial white stuff is gone, resist the urge to keep squeezing and bruise your face. Instead, clean the area with a cotton ball soaked in alcohol and apply a small dab of facial "mud," often called a facial "mask," available at most drugstores. The mud will suck out the remaining liquid and help the blemish heal overnight.

Facial mud can also help bring down blemishes that you have not drained, and is generally less drying than over-the-counter acne lotions.

The next morning, apply a small amount of light moisturizer to help the affected area heal. Do not attempt to drain your blemishes if your skin is prone to scarring.

Avoid cysts. If you develop a large, hard blemish with no white-head, or a whitehead that fails to yield a proportionate amount of puss, *leave it alone*. You may have an acne cyst that will not respond to squeezing, but will eventually recede. Alternatively, visit a dermatologist for a faster remedy.

Getting more help. Of course, not all acne is the product of poor skin care; see a dermatologist if your skin does not respond to consistent cleaning.

THE GROOMING ISSUE:
ACNE SCARRING & PITTING

THE FACTS:

Some teen and adult acne leaves scarring and deep pitting long after the blemishes are gone.

THE GROOMING SOLUTION:

If you find that your skin scars easily, refrain from picking at your blemishes to avoid further scarring.

Too late? One way to "smooth" out skin and reduce the effects of scarring is to generate new skin growth with a chemical agent that peels away the uppermost layers of the skin. As new skin develops, the appearance of top-layer scarring is reduced. Obviously, no over-the-counter product is strong enough to do this safely. If you're interested in this treatment, visit a dermatologist for a consultation on a "chemical peel" or on "laser resurfacing."

THE GROOMING ISSUE:
BLOTCHY RED SKIN OR ROSACEA

THE FACTS:

Have you developed red blotches on your face that you cannot attribute to normal acne or dryness? You may have *rosacea,* a condition where blood vessels at the upper layers of your skin burst and cause the skin to appear red and splotchy.

Early symptoms include recurrent flushing and blushing, lasting several minutes or several hours. Other signs include stinging in the forehead region or ears.

Severe rosacea may even cause you to develop pustules (i.e., whiteheads) and severe inflammation, which is why it is often misdiagnosed as acne. *Very* severe rosacea is accompanied by a condition called *rhinophyma,* an enlargement of the nose and the thickening of the skin tissue in that area. While rosacea is more common in women, SharpMen who suffer from rosacea develop much more severe symptoms.

THE GROOMING SOLUTION:

Rosacea cannot be treated at home. If you believe you have this skin condition, see a dermatologist for diagnosis and the benefit of professional treatment. Many products recommended for this condition contain *salicylic acid,* a chemical exfoliant that reduces irritation and redness in the skin by generating new skin growth. Rosacea may also be treated by laser and cauterizing treatments.

THE GROOMING ISSUE:
BROWN SPOTS & WRINKLING

THE FACTS:

Some skin problems are self-inflicted. Prime examples are brown spots (or "age spots") and wrinkling on your face and neck. As it turns out, eighty percent of facial surface deterioration is caused by voluntary and involuntary exposure to the sun. Think your worker-bee schedule makes you immune? Think again. The average SharpMan traveling from home to work and back can become exposed to over eighteen hours of damaging UVA and UVB rays *per week*.

> ## REQUIRED GEAR
> ———•••••———
> • Sunscreen, SPF 15 or higher.

And while younger guys may not consider what the sun does to their future mugs during a ball game (that's women's territory, right?), if they care about their outward appearance, they should. As women become more savvy about the benefits of sun protection, many SharpMen linger far behind, refusing to use sunscreens or make use of other sun protection under the assumption that brown spots and saggy skin will make then look *distinguished*.

The real question is; will a big chunk removed from your face (a common treatment for melanoma) also make you look distinguished? Protect yourself from sun damage to avoid not-so-distinguished growths and other forms of skin cancer.

THE GROOMING SOLUTION:

The good news is that sun damage is the easiest skin problem to prevent. Simply wear sunscreen daily, preferably SPF 15 or higher.

Want more good news? Products that contain Vitamin C and wheat whey may slightly reverse the aging process when used regularly – including brown spots and wrinkling. These treatments firm up the texture of your skin, and if you're exfoliating, the pigment of your brown spots may lighten over time. Speak to your dermatologist about the use of these supplements.

THE GROOMING ISSUE: Cold Sores

THE FACTS:

It's hard to feel confident with a big blister on your lip. Cold sores, often called fever blisters, are caused by a common, contagious viral infection called *herpes one*. The infection causes blisters on the lips, around the mouth and occasionally on the gums. The blisters fill with fluid, dry up and then heal over. If left untreated, a cold sore will take anywhere from four to ten days to clear up, but the virus remains in your system, often lying dormant for some time before another cold sore appears.

Stress, colds, flu, sunburn, eating certain nuts or coming in contact with someone who has an active cold sore can all cause a blister breakout. That's when your battle begins.

REQUIRED GEAR

For prevention:
• Lip balm with SPF 15 or higher.
• Over-the-counter or prescription creams and ointments.
• Prescription oral medication.
For treatment:
• Over-the-counter or prescription creams, ointments and pills.

THE GROOMING SOLUTION:

Your ideal solution is to arrest the breakout of a blister *before* it reaches the skin surface. Often this is possible by simply treating your lips in time.

How do you do this most effectively?

Identify the start. Begin by identifying the early symptoms. Most cold sore sufferers will first feel a tingling, burning or itching sensation in the area on or around their lips. While the application of an over-the-counter product may help, seeing your dermatologist for prescription medication may be more effective.

Avoid breakouts. Once you've been infected, as with other forms of illness, the frequency and severity of breakouts largely depend on your stress level and general health. By learning to manage your reaction to stress, you may be able to inhibit breakouts or even control the beginning of a breakout. Some physicians advise closing your eyes, breathing slowly and deeply and envisioning your blister shrinking back into your skin. At the same time, help boost your immune system by drinking fluids, eating well and getting an ample amount of sleep.

It also helps to reduce the circumstances that promote breakouts. It you feel a sore coming on, keep the affected area out of the sun by wearing a hat and a lip balm with SPF 15 or higher. Many doctors also advise patients to avoid eating nuts, a common aggravator.

See a physician. If your efforts to prevent a breakout prove futile, the correct treatment can speed up your healing process significantly. At the very least, you'll want to reduce the discomfort as much as possible. See a dermatologist for strong prescription medication.

Reduce the pain. You can minimize cold sore discomfort by drinking cold drinks and avoiding spicy or salty foods. Placing an ice cube against the cold sore during the first twenty-four hours of a breakout can prevent swelling of the lip.

Avoid spreading. Don't scratch or pick at your sore. Doing so may irritate the wound (prolonging the breakout) or cause the infection to spread to other areas of your lips or mouth.

If you do touch your sore, refrain from touching your eyes and face and promptly wash your hands. During and after your infection, try to change your towels, washcloths and pillowcases more frequently to avoid further spread and recurrent breakouts.

SHARPNOTE: Never had a cold sore? Initial infection generally occurs when you come into contact with another infected person. For this reason, avoid kissing or otherwise coming into contact with someone who has an active blister. Also avoid drinking from the same glass or using the same towel as anyone with a visible sore. Note that while highly contagious, particularly at the early stage of the sore, infection is unlikely to be spread in the absence of a visible breakout.

THE GROOMING ISSUE:
FACIAL COSMETIC SURGERY FOR GUYS

THE FACTS:

While altering one's outward appearance — especially surgically — is by no means required of any SharpMan, those guys who *are* curious about doing so are no less sharp. After all, if it makes you feel better, why not?

THE GROOMING SOLUTION:

Facial surgery aims to make you look younger, or — if you are already young — correct or reshape certain facial elements. For example, think your ears stick out too far? Ear pinning can tuck them in a bit closer to your hairline. Did your teen years leave your skin looking like the surface of the moon? Laser resurfacing can smooth out the indentations of acne scarring. Think you have a "weak" chin? Chin implants can reshape the silhouette of your jaw line.

Of course, facial surgery also includes facelifts, neck lifts, eyelid work, brow lifts, forehead lifts and nose jobs.

The more minor facial surgery techniques are hardly "surgery" at all. Some procedures, like ear pinning, can be quickly performed during your lunch break. Healing time depends on you, but the localized "tender" feeling should cease within a couple of weeks.

More intensive procedures — like all-out facelifts — require a hospital visit and recovery time.

For men who want the big jobs, the hair growth on your scalp and face will determine where the least conspicuous surgical incisions can be made. If you have thinning hair or a high hairline, special surgical artistry may be used to hide incisions.

Also, be aware that men have a richer blood supply in their facial areas and are therefore more likely than women to bleed during surgery. Men are also at greater risk of having blood temporarily collect under the skin following surgery, causing greater bruising.

Finally, consider that you may have to wait up to three weeks following more serious facial surgery before shaving again, and that drinking alcohol in the weeks following surgery can cause the treated areas to become red or flushed.

To find out more about the variety of procedures available to men, contact your dermatologist or physician for a referral. For a more anonymous referral, contact an association of plastic surgeons in your area.

THE GROOMING ISSUE: EAR CARE 101

THE FACTS:

Most SharpMen don't think about ear maintenance until they hear complaints from their T.V.-watching buddies: "Turn that down; are you deaf or something?" This exchange is usually followed by a brief — but fleeting — thought

> ### REQUIRED GEAR
>
> • Soap.
> • Washcloth.
> • Cotton swabs.

about ear cleaning. In reality, most guys refrain from cleaning their ears because they (a) don't know how, and (b) may have heard that cleaning ears improperly could lead to hearing damage.

THE GROOMING SOLUTION:

Think it's time to clean your ears? If so, recognize that not all ear wax should be removed.

Ear wax is important: it serves as the cleaning mechanism of the ear canal. It traps dust in the inner canal and then removes the dust (along with itself) to the outer ear – the part you can reach into with your finger.

For this reason, there's no point in reaching in and digging out the build-up in your inner ear. In most cases, this mass of wax will make its own way out. It *is* a good idea to clean out the opening of the ear (the part that protrudes from your head), but stop there. Just use a washcloth and mild soap to clean the outer ear while you shower. This is the *only* part of your ear you should *ever* touch with a cotton swab.

As for using cotton swabs, avoid sticking them into your ear canal far as they'll reach. This pushes more wax into the ear than it removes. You also run the risk of scratching the ear canal or even damaging your ear drum. Use a fresh side of the cotton swab for each of your ears.

Sometimes excess wax does accumulate in your ear. Often, this occurs because you've been too zealous with your cotton swab and crammed the wax back into your ear canal. This build-up is most safely removed by an ear nose and throat ("ENT") physician. Home kits are also available for occasional use, but should never be used in lieu of seeing a physician.

THE GROOMING ISSUE:
COMBATING BAD BREATH

THE FACTS:

Most SharpMen may not realize the strong connection between failing to floss and stinky breath. Anytime you eat or drink, small particles of food lodge themselves between your teeth. What's that? You say that you *always* brush? Brushing removes *only* those particles of food that lie on the *surface* of your teeth, whereas food and other smelly substances trapped between the teeth just sit there – rotting – *almost as if you had never bothered to brush at all.* The result is some seriously stinky breath.

REQUIRED GEAR

- Waxed floss "string" for teeth spaced close together.
- Waxed floss "tape," also known as "dental tape" for teeth with gaps between them.
- Mouthwash or breath mints.
- Parsley or oral products containing parsley.

THE GROOMING SOLUTION:

If you believe your mouth is a party to this level of stink, then flossing is for you. The following quick flossing tips will help you do the job without damaging your gums:

Step One: Floss before you brush. This way you ensure that the particles you removed from in between your teeth are brushed and rinsed away.

Step Two: Use enough floss. Use approximately 12 to 18 inches of floss and wind an end of the floss around the middle finger of each hand, leaving roughly one inch of floss between the fingertips.

Step Three: Saw gently. Use a gentle sawing motion to insert floss just in between your teeth—but be careful not to jerk the floss "knife" into your gums.

Step Four: Bend as you saw. Slowly bring the floss towards the gum line, then bend the floss on both sides, so that it curves into a "c" shape against the sides of your tooth. Use an up-and-down scraping motion to remove plaque just beneath the gum line and in between teeth.

Step Five: Repeat. Repeat step four on the next tooth, between all of your teeth and behind your molars, as well. Use a different one-inch portion of the floss each time you floss.

SHARPNOTE: What about coffee and garlic stink? Because it's not always possible to brush and floss after you eat and drink, arming your pocket or desk drawer with a few tricks of the good-breath trade can be helpful for evenings out or days at the office:

Coffee stink. "Shallow" bad breath, such as coffee stink, only affects your tongue and mouth. These superficial bad breath brands can be easily combated with mints or mouthwash.

Garlic stink. And if you had garlic for lunch or dinner? Garlic and other food smells emanate from your *digestive system,* not your mouth, so no number of mints will be enough to mask the odor for longer than the mint is in your mouth. The age-old remedy for neutralizing digestive odors is parsley. Ever wonder why it's always on the edge of your plate? It isn't just for garnish. So go ahead and munch on the green stuff at the end of your meal. Alternatively, most drugstores stock parsley pills for easy desk or pocket access after meals.

THE GROOMING ISSUE: TEETH WHITENING

THE FACTS:

Teeth can become stained for a number of reasons, the most common being consumption of coffee, tea, berries, fruit juices, smoking, and just plain-old aging. In other words, simply being a normal human being can cause your teeth to yellow.

The good news is that stained teeth can be safely whitened or bleached.

THE GROOMING SOLUTION:

When considering whether to whiten your teeth, skip the infomercials and visit your dentist. He or she will check out your mouth to ensure that it's healthy enough to bleach safely and to determine whether cosmetic whitening is appropriate for you.

Who can bleach? Some teeth bleach better than others. Yellow teeth generally respond to treatment, while brownish or grayish teeth (caused by tetracycline use) are unlikely to bleach well. In some cases porcelain veneers or dental bonding may be more suitable. A dental consultation is particularly important for SharpMen with fillings or crowns.

Safety first. Is bleaching gel safe? The most common active ingredient in bleaching gel is ten percent *carbamide peroxide,* which breaks down into three percent *hydrogen peroxide* when dispensed. It's been used for years and is considered safe, *especially under a dentist's supervision.*

It's a go. If your dentist determines that cosmetic bleaching is for you, he or she will make impressions of your teeth and create custom mouth guard trays for you. To protect your sensitive gum tissue, he or she will leave a slight space between the tray and your gums when forming the tray.

The how-tos. Depending on your particular discoloration and gum sensitivity, your dentist will instruct you on the proper use of mouth guards and bleaching gel. Treatments generally last between one week to one month. Your dentist will also likely ask you to come in for a reevaluation during your treatment to ensure that your bleaching is progressing safely.

Use in moderation. Avoid using more gel or wearing your mouth guards longer than your dentist recommends. If you experience any pain in your teeth or gums, contact your dentist immediately.

Side effects. The most common side effect associated with bleaching is tooth sensitivity. Generally, this side effect is mild and temporary, lasting only as long as your bleaching treatment. Gum irritation is uncommon and generally associated with improper use of guard trays.

Repeat customers. The effects of cosmetic bleaching should last indefinitely, that is, so long as you avoid staining foods and beverages and maintain good oral health. That means brushing at least twice a day, flossing, and visiting your dentist every six months for a thorough cleaning and check-up.

On the other hand, if you continue to ingest those items that stained your teeth in the first place, your teeth *will* gradually yellow again. Luckily, it's safe to repeat bleaching under a dentist's supervision.

SHARPNOTE: Many over-the-counter whitening toothpastes can *slowly* help remove surface stains and keep yellowing from returning once you've had it bleached away. Unfortunately, on their own, whitening toothpastes will not yield the quick, dramatic changes found with bleaching.

SHAMPOOING 101

SHARPCUTS
> Better Cuts for Your Hair Type
> Better Cuts for Your Face Type

YOUR HAIR AT WORK
> Cuts for Day & Night
> Job Interview & Date Hair

SHARPHAIR MAINTENANCE
> Making Your Cut Last
> Hair Junk
> Combating Frizz
> Straightening Curly Hair
> Long Hair Care

HAIR ISSUES
> Dandruff
> Hair Loss
> Comb-overs
> Wind-sensitive Hair
> Gray Hair

THE GROOMING ISSUE: SHAMPOOING 101

THE FACTS:

In general, men's hair comes in three types: oily, dry or damaged. Each of these require SharpMen to wash and condition their hair differently in order to achieve the best results.

THE GROOMING SOLUTION:

Oily hair. If you find your hair to be generally oily or greasy, avoid running your hands through your hair. Despite how suave the gesture, simply putting your hands in contact with your hair transfers oil from your skin, adding oil to an already slick surface.

When it comes to washing oily hair, the drill is simple: read the front of your shampoo bottle. Choose shampoos designed specifically for oily — and often "smooth" — hair.   On the other hand, despite the "rinse and repeat" instruction on the back, only shampoo your hair *once* and skip the conditioner.   If you find that your hair requires a bit of moisture in the winter months, limit conditioning to a once-a-week treatment.

> ### REQUIRED GEAR
>
> • Shampoo for your hair type.
> • Conditioner for your hair type.

Dry hair. If your hair doesn't feel oily in between washes and tends to look frazzled at the ends, it may require a bit of moisture. This is especially true for guys who spend a lot of time in the water or in the sun. Sure, it may look ratty to you, but dry and brittle hair is easy to manage.

To care for dry, coarse hair, find a shampoo specifically designed for this hair type. Because dry hair requires a natural build-up of scalp oil to keep it looking good, only use your dry hair shampoo every *couple* of days. Go ahead and shower daily, but skip the hair wash. On the other hand, use a good conditioner *every time* you shower — whether you shampoo or not. It may sound strange, but simply letting conditioner sit on wet, unwashed hair for a few minutes will make styling your locks that much easier.

Damaged hair. SharpMen who try bringing their look up a notch with bleaching or color treatments can inadvertently damage their hair. Color, bleach and similar products are pretty harsh. Drugstore home treatments are even worse. For this reason, consider splurging on a professional color or bleaching treatment. Products used by the pros are easier on hair, and professional stylists are less likely to damage your hair by keeping the product on too long.

For washing at home, ask your hairstylist to recommend a shampoo specially designed for color- or bleach-treated hair. You'll find that these products make your hair look shinier, assist in styling and maintain the color much longer than other shampoos. Of course, better-lasting color means you thrash your hair less often and save money on fewer repeat treatments.

Another way to lengthen the time between treatments is to find a "color enhancing" shampoo. These shampoos actually add your preferred color as you use them.

Because color is so tough on hair, follow your shampoo with a conditioning treatment designed for color-treated or damaged hair.

SHARPNOTE: Is it necessary to spring for expensive salon shampoos and conditioners for hair that is not color-treated or bleached? Not really. Often you'll find that your hair responds just as well to drugstore brands.

THE GROOMING ISSUE:
MATCHING YOUR CUT TO YOUR HAIR TYPE

THE FACTS:

We've all had them: the bad haircut and the ensuing bad hair days (or *months*). Consider the connection between the two and avoid both by picking a style that suits your type of hair. That's right. Long before you step up to the barber's chair, you can determine what haircuts will best flatter your type of hair.

THE GROOMING SOLUTION:

Straight hair. Straight hair often lacks the volume to support high altitude hairstyles. For this reason, a simple cut is your best bet. Try a 1940s style with hair cropped short on the sides and back, front parted to the side. Avoid "cookie-cutter" haircuts, where the hair on the back and sides of your head is cut above the hairline. Helpful styling products for straight hair? Try a "volumizing" mousse or gel designed to give more bang to your straight hair buck.

Light to medium curly hair. While less problematic than super-curls, light to medium curls require special attention. The sides and back should be short and tight, with the hair cut above the ears. The less curl in your hair, the longer you can go with your cut on top. But avoid letting all that length go to your head. Growing your hair too long on the top and sides can leave you looking like a poodle. Too long in the back and you'll be back in the early 1980s – but not in a good way.

To define your curls and avoid frizz, try a soft setting gel. To control and style without curl definition, use a strong gel or pomade. With

---

REQUIRED GEAR

--•=◆=•--

- *Straight hair:* volumizing mousse or gel.
- *Light to medium curly hair:* pomade, soft setting or strong hold gel.
- *Super curly hair:* setting gel.
- *Fine or thinning hair:* volumizing mousse or gel.
- Blow-dryer.

a quarter-sized amount of either product in your palm, rub hands together and apply, working into the hair with your fingertips.

Super curly hair. There are many casual ways to wear super-curly hair, such as the "afro," long tresses on all or two sides, or dread-locks. For a cut suitable for most working (read: "dating") environments, one strong style stands out for turbo-curly hair: cut hair one-fourth of an inch short all over, so that your entire head of hair is one length. Never comb out longer curly hair to avoid frizz.

To reproduce this look at home, ask your stylist to recommend a setting gel. With a quarter-sized amount of the product in your palm, rub hands together and apply, working into hair with your fingertips.

Fine hair. Fine hair can appear fuller if styled correctly. Request a short cut that pushes your hair forward. This allows each hair to cover more of your scalp, thereby making your hair look thicker than it is. Avoid cuts that call for you to comb hair sideways or back, as they highlight the fact that your hair is fine.

When styling, thicken hair by applying a half-dollar sized amount of volumizing mousse or gel to your entire head of hair. Work the product through your hair with your hands. Using a medium-heat blow-dryer, blow hair in all directions until dry, thereby giving the appearance of fuller, thicker hair.

Thinning hair. Hair that is thinning around the front hairline (not at the back or crown of your head) is treated similarly to fine hair, with special attention paid to the sides of your front hairline, where your hair is receding. As with fine hair, comb forward, taking emphasis off the receding hairline. As for the best cut, keep it cropped fairly short on top and sides, no more than one to one and a half inches long. Avoid adhering flat, thinning hair to the scalp, or growing one side longer for the "comb-over." In other words, keep it short and ignore it. You'll be seen as sharper for it.

When styling, thicken hair by applying a half-dollar sized amount of volumizing mousse or gel to your entire head of hair. Work product through hair with your hands. Using a medium-heat blow-dryer, blow hair in all directions until dry, thereby giving the appearance of fuller, thicker hair.

SHARPNOTE ONE: Great hair days begin with great haircuts and *practice*. Take time to get to know your hair and what it can and *can't* do. Don't fight Mother Nature – go with what you have naturally so that your style won't look "strained." Remember that men have no mandate to change hairstyles with the seasons. Find and stick to what works for you.

SHARPNOTE TWO: A common misconception dictates that blow-drying is required for a great hair day. Blow-dryers are not always necessary. For shorter hairstyles, towel dry first, then apply your hair product and allow the hair to dry naturally. Don't plug in unless the product instructions call for it.

THE GROOMING ISSUE:
MATCHING YOUR CUT TO YOUR FACE

THE FACTS:

In addition to matching your haircut to your hair type, matching your cut to the shape of your face or those facial features you'd like to downplay is another way to get more bang for your hairstyle buck.

THE GROOMING SOLUTION:

Round faces. To de-emphasize your round baby face, consider a style that moves hair away from your mug. Avoid cuts that require full hair on the sides. To add length and height to your face, consider a style with longer hair on top.

Thin faces. To make your face look fuller and avoid a long, thin look, avoid hairstyles with "height." Instead, speak to your stylist about a cut that is fuller on the sides.

Protruding ears. To take attention away from large or protruding ears, speak to your stylist about a cut that is longer on the sides. Fuller styles that creep up over the ears look best, if the shape of your face allows.

Substantial noses. If you feel self-conscious about your nose, avoid super-short cuts, as these tend to draw attention to all strong features.

Facial scars. If you'd like to mask scarring at the top or sides of your face, your stylist may be able to recommend a cut and style to obscure this feature. For centrally located scarring, consider one of several facial hair styles. See the *Choosing Facial Hair to Flatter the Shape of Your Face* section of this guidebook for more information. Neither option suits your style? Just ignore your scarring and you'll find that most everyone else will eventually do the same.

SHARPNOTE: Ready for a big change? Going from long to short hair can be a bit drastic. By the same token, gradually going from short to sloppy to long can be excruciatingly slow. How can you ease these transitions?

Short to long. To avoid looking sloppy during your short-to-long transition, consider growing the top part of your hair before growing out the sides.

Long to short. If you'd like to shorten your hair but aren't sure what length or look you'll ultimately settle on, try cutting in stages.

THE GROOMING ISSUE: Getting 24/7 Hair

THE FACTS:

Often SharpMen's day jobs and night lives require different looks. If you're a corporate stiff by day who enjoys loosening up at night and on the weekends, finding a double-duty haircut is your best bet.

THE GROOMING SOLUTION:

Straight or wavy hair. Consider a short cut – as short as your hair will go before it spikes up on its own, but long enough to lie flat when combed down into a more conservative style. Use a small amount of mousse to comb hair back into your daytime look. Once you've punched out for the day, apply a quarter-sized amount of strong hold gel or a dime-sized amount of pomade to your palm. Rub your hands together and use your fingers to pinch small clumps of your hair into different directions for a more casual evening style.

REQUIRED GEAR

• *Straight or wavy hair:* mousse for day; strong hold gel or pomade for after hours.
• *Curly or frizzy hair:* strong hold gel or pomade for day; setting gel for after hours.

Curly or frizzy hair. Ask your stylist for a cut short enough to comb back for work and long enough to show off your Sampson-like curls after hours. Try a cut approximately two inches long all around. To style for day, use a strong hold gel or pomade to comb hair back. For evenings and weekends, apply a quarter-sized amount of setting gel onto your palm, rub hands together and apply to your curls but not your roots. Work the product into your hair with your fingertips to define (read: de-frizz) your curls and overall look.

THE GROOMING ISSUE: INTERVIEW & DATE HAIR

THE FACTS:

Can a "good hair day" make a difference on a big interview or date? Studies indicate that to the extent a great hair day makes you feel more attractive, it will also make you feel more confident and positively affect your interactions with others. Hoping to project your best despite the nerves? In addition to practicing your smooth moves and patented interview answers, take a moment to get that quaff under control.

THE GROOMING SOLUTION:

Step One: Schedule a haircut. Instruct your stylist to take off less, rather than more. Prudence will avoid a last-minute disaster.

Step Two: Invest in a few of those hair-care products your stylist keeps trying to push off on you. Then spend a few more minutes having him or her teach you exactly how to apply and blow-dry for game day. Don't be shy — *it's your cash.* Don't leave until you feel confident that you have a solid understanding of how to re-create the look yourself.

Step Three: Practice. In the days before the event, make a habit of taking time to practice the routine. Like baseball or that musical instrument your mother always wanted you to play, you'll never get good unless you work the steps.

Step Four: Allow for prep time. Make a point of waking up earlier on the day of the date or interview, and leave yourself a nice cushion of time in which to redo your "do" as needed.

THE GROOMING ISSUE:
MAKING YOUR HAIRCUT LAST

THE FACTS:

Man, is it time for another haircut already? It seems like just the other week you were taking time out of your schedule to get a trim and fork out the cash. Take heart. With a few SharpMan tips, you can maintain your look longer and minimize your trips to the chair.

THE GROOMING SOLUTION:

Step One: Keep your back hairline neat. One of the tell-tale signs of a required trim is the messy hairline on the back of your head, at the top of your neck. If you maintain this line on your own, you'll be able to put off the full deal for several weeks. Invest in a non-professional version of the electric clippers used by your stylist. Attach the length accessory and adjust it to the shortest setting. With your electric clippers in hand, stand in front of a wall mirror, grab a hand mirror, turn around and look at the back of your head. With the clipper in your most adept hand, run it over the hairline area. *Don't cut into your existing hairline.* Simply follow the line that you see. Trim your neckline once a week.

Step Two: Keep the back of your neck clean.

REQUIRED GEAR

• Electric trimmer with length attachment.
• Hand mirror.
• Mustache comb.
• Mustache scissors (i.e., short and straight).

Another haircut alarm? A hairy neck and back. To clean this up yourself, stand in front of a wall mirror, grab your hand mirror and turn around. Use your electric clippers to shave off the hair on your neck and back below the hairline you just cleaned up. Again, be careful not to alter the hairline itself. Trim accordingly every two to four weeks.

Step Three: *Clean up those sideburns.* Get yourself a good pair of mustache scissors (i.e., short, straight and sharp). Stand in front of a wall mirror with your shears in one hand and a small narrow-toothed mustache comb in the other. Comb each sideburn back towards your ears and then forward until you see the intended hairline of the sideburn and the scraggly pieces of hair that have grown long enough to mess up the line. With your scissors facing up towards your sideburn at a 45 degree angle, cut off these odd pieces using small choppy cuts. Target only one or two hairs per cut until you have cleaned up the entire sideburn. Trim your sideburns once a week.

THE GROOMING ISSUE: USING HAIR JUNK

THE FACTS:

Just as different hair types call for different washing routines, matching your hair type – oily, dry or damaged – with the right styling aids can make it easier to look your best.

THE GROOMING SOLUTION:

Oily hair. Styling oily hair can be a challenge. Most styling products contain agents that, if applied in excess, will make your hair even oilier. If you believe your hair is oily, avoid pomades, oily gels, styling creams and lotions. Opt for mousses, hair spray and "texturizing" products. Regardless of the styling products you choose, always use styling agents in moderation. Apply a dime-sized amount to your palm, rub your hands together and apply only half of the product in your hands to the ends of your hair. To avoid a greasy look, don't apply the product to your roots or scalp. If you find that you need more hair junk for your look, add small amounts in parts. After all, it's always easier to add product than to hop back into the shower and start over.

REQUIRED GEAR

- Hair spray, mousses and "texturizing" lotion for oily hair.
- Gels, pomades, styling lotions and creams for dry hair.

Dry or damaged hair. SharpMen with dry hair should avoid mousses, hair sprays or gels not specifically designed for their hair type. Otherwise you'll find that the alcohol in these products will make your hair even more dry and hard to style. Opt for styling lotions, pomades, creams or "moisturizing" mousses. Apply a small quarter-sized amount of product to your palms, rub your hands together and apply at the ends of your hair – the driest areas that cause that "flyaway" look. Add small amounts of styling product as needed to avoid flaking.

In-between hair. If your hair is neither clearly oily nor dry, experiment with the products your hairstylist recommends. If you find that your hair flakes when you use gels, hair sprays or mousses, switch to light pomades, creams or lotions. Apply small amounts to the ends of your hair to avoid a greasy look.

SHARPNOTE: The sheer number of products on the market makes choosing a hairstyling aid confusing. To make matters worse, hair products seem to come in and out of "fashion." Should you care? Not really. Forget the fads and stick with what works for you.

THE GROOMING ISSUE: COMBATING FRIZZY HAIR

THE FACTS:

Whether curly or straight, some SharpMen's hair has a mind of its own. To avoid having your hair fly in all directions after a wash, consider using a hairstyling product made with *silica*. Silica is a plastic incorporated into styling products designed to control frizzy hair.

THE GROOMING SOLUTION:

To use a silica-based product to control out-of-control frizz, apply a small amount to the palm of your hand, rub your palms together and apply small amounts to the ends, roots and some hair in between. Rather than applying to individual hairs, grab small "clumps" of hair when you apply. As with all products, start by using less than you think you need and add as you go.

REQUIRED GEAR

- Silica-based hair product.

THE GROOMING ISSUE:
STRAIGHTENING CURLY LOCKS

THE FACTS:

Curly hair is hard to fight. Think your hair is too curly for its own good? Has styling (read: controlling) your curly hair become a losing battle? Consider one of several processes for straightening curly hair.

THE GROOMING SOLUTION:

Blow-drying. It is possible to "blow out" curly hair with a round brush and a blow-dryer. When you step out of the shower, towel dry your hair and apply a mousse or setting gel. Begin brushing out your hair with the round brush, holding and working the brush below the hair as you zap it with the blow-dryer. It takes patience, but your hair will eventually give in – until your next shower, that is.

Chemical straightening. If blowing out your hair isn't an option, consider having your hair chemically straightened. This is kind of like a reverse perm — the process *unwinds* hair instead of winding. Like any chemical process, chemical straightening must be done by a professional. If too much tension is placed on the hair while the straightening lotion is on, your hair could break off. If the lotion is left on too long, your hair could dissolve. In other words, don't try this at home.

When choosing a stylist to straighten your hair, ensure that he or she has experience with chemical straightening. Additionally, unless "bald" is your look, always request that your stylist use a "neutralizer" — key to protecting your hair during this harsh process.

Chemical relaxing. Alternatively, consider having your hair "relaxed" by a professional. The key to this process is timing. Once your hairstylist applies the relaxant, he or she must style your hair exactly the way you intend to wear it after the treatment. The hair will break down into this shape. Because this process requires precision, make a point of checking that the stylist you choose is experienced with relaxers and understands the hairstyle you have in mind *before* the treatment is applied.

And again, despite your buddies' "great" idea after a night of partying, always go to a professional. Cheapo over-the-counter products left on just a few minutes too long can cause hair to break and may leave you with bald patches.

SHARPNOTE: If you're trying to get "body" out of your chemical treatment, skip the perm. Consider using a thickening gel instead. Choose a product made with a lot of alcohol for maximum effect. Despite the fact that the alcohol is damaging to your hair, it will be a lot less damaging than a perm. Plus, the benefit of using hair junk over a permanent treatment is that you can wash it out when you're ready for a new look.

THE GROOMING ISSUE: MAINTAINING LONG HAIR

THE FACTS:

While easier on the wallet, long hair requires more maintenance than shorter styles. After all, you generally have to take better care of the stuff you want to keep for a longer period of time. What's more, neglected long hair shows it.

REQUIRED GEAR

- Shampoo.
- Conditioner.
- Detangling spray.
- Leave-in conditioning lotion.

If you find that your hair becomes more unruly and harder to style as it grows, your locks may be in need of some extra help.

THE GROOMING SOLUTION:

To keep your long hair looking its best, take better care of the ends. When the ends become dry or are brushed too roughly, they tend to break and split (i.e., "split ends"). Why should you care? Because split ends cause your mane to thin and look, well, *ratty*.

Step One: Condition. To prevent this, consider using a conditioner after you shampoo. Apply the conditioner to the part of your hair that hangs below your ears all the way down to your ends. There's no need to use conditioner on your scalp and roots. Simply wipe off the excess conditioner from your hands onto this area. Let the product soak in for a few minutes while you soap up. Rinse your hair and towel dry.

Step Two: Detangle. Before laying into your hair with that chainsaw you call a hairbrush, spray on a detangling product. Detangling sprays prevent hair from snagging and breaking as you brush.

Step Three: Brush and lube. Begin by brushing out the ends and then work up to your scalp. Don't be rough; be patient. Follow with another "leave on" conditioning lotion, but only at the ends. This helps prevent that thrashed, "fly-away" look and makes your hair easier to style. Make a point of having your hair trimmed every two months or so to keep your ends from looking fried.

THE GROOMING ISSUE:
DEALING WITH DANDRUFF

THE FACTS:

Sure dandruff isn't the *worst* thing that could happen to a guy, but having white flakes sprinkling down your shoulders isn't exactly the Time Magazine® Man of the Year look.

Dandruff is actually a form of *eczema* that causes skin to flake on the scalp, but can also affect facial hair, chest hair, ears, and any area of the body

> # REQUIRED GEAR
>
> • Dandruff shampoo or prescription treatment.

where skin comes in contact with other skin (i.e., underarms, inner elbows, behind the knees and in the groin). Dandruff flaking can also cause itching and occasional redness.

The cause of dandruff is unknown, although the tendency to develop it is hereditary. Dandruff can have both active and inactive periods; remaining invisible for months between flare-ups. It often affects SharpMen with oily skin and may leave skin looking greasy or unclean.

Because there is no known cure for dandruff, your best bet is to put your efforts towards *prevention.* Luckily, dandruff can be controlled by any number of relatively inexpensive and easy-to-use treatments.

THE GROOMING SOLUTION:

Over-the-counter shampoos. Dandruff control can be as close as your local drugstore. These over-the-counter treatments differ from conventional shampoos in that they contain ingredients like *salicylic acid, coal tar, selenium sulfide, pyrithione zinc,* or *sulfur.* They may sound a bit fierce, but they're actually safe, gentle and appropriate for all hair types. When properly used, they greatly minimize dandruff flare-ups in all but the most severe cases.

While dandruff sufferers should shampoo daily, dandruff shampoos aren't designed to be used every day. Alternate your medicinal shampoo with your regular hair product, using your dandruff treatment every second or third washing.

If you find that one dandruff shampoo doesn't stop your flaking, consider picking up another product with a different active ingredient. Try several shampoos to determine which ingredient your scalp responds to best.

For beard dandruff, try lathering your facial hair up with dandruff shampoo once a week. Allow the shampoo to soak in for five minutes before rinsing.

Prescription lotions. Occasionally a case of dandruff will not respond to over-the-counter treatments. If you've tried several shampoos and haven't seen a decrease in flaking, see your doctor – preferably a dermatologist – who can examine your noggin and prescribe special scalp lotions. Prescription dandruff lotions often contain *selenium, corticosteroids* or *ketaconazole (Nizoral*™*)*, powerful ingredients that help control scalp flaking.

Environmental controls. Dandruff can also become aggravated by a number of outside factors. In some cases, dry scalp skin and dandruff are related to stress, fatigue, infrequent shampooing, hair products containing alcohol (check out the ingredient list on your gel), tight-fitting or non-breathable hats and failing to dry hair and skin completely after showering. In the case of these aggravators, a few simple lifestyle changes can make a big difference.

Another tip? Participating in outdoor activities during warm weather also seems to reduce dandruff outbreaks. *So play ball!*

SharpThreads for dandruff. Got dandruff? To minimize the evidence of your outbreak, consider wearing light colors. Lighter colors, especially white, can be somewhat effective in camouflaging dandruff flakes, whereas dark colors call attention to the winter wonderland on your shoulders.

SHARPNOTE ONE: It is common for dandruff shampoos to become less effective over time. If your shampoo of choice has lost its juice, simply switch to another one, and switch again when your second choice peters out.

SHARPNOTE TWO: While uncommon, some SharpMen's skin may become sensitive to one or more of the ingredients found in medicinal shampoos. If your skin becomes red after using one of these treatments, immediately discontinue use and consult your physician.

THE GROOMING ISSUE:
MAXIMIZING ON THINNING HAIR

THE FACTS:

While a natural genetic occurrence for many men, thinning hair-lines are not always "naturally" accepted by men and mainstream culture. Because of this, some SharpMen who discover that they are losing their hair also experience anxiety and a relative loss of self-esteem.

Why does male hair loss occur?

Contrary to what many people believe, male-pattern baldness can be inherited from either parent. The hair loss trait is prone to skipping generations and may even skip or favor one sibling over another. While genes are important, outside factors, including diet, illness, tobacco use and hair care habits can also play a role. In addition, hairstyles that pull on hair, such as ponytails and braids, can affect or expedite hair loss, as can consistently wearing and removing a baseball cap.

THE GROOMING SOLUTION:

Miracle cures abound. Every year brings a new product, pill, or surgical procedure promising to re-grow all or part of the hair men lose. With so many choices, how do you decide on a hair treatment method? The best advice is to consult your doctor or dermatologist before trying any method, since different chemical factors may manifest themselves uniquely in different SharpMen. *In other words, what grows hair for some may promote hair loss in others.*

For SharpMen who don't care for tonics, shampoos or pills, check out these options:

Hair transplantations. The most popular procedure for hair transplantation is the graft — a surgical procedure that borrows hair from an abundantly hairy area of your head or body and transplants it onto an area that requires more. A successful procedure will partially fill in a balding area and result in a fuller hairline. Unfortunately, grafting is unlikely to reproduce the full head of hair you had as a kid. This treatment method is relatively safe, with less than one percent of all cases resulting in post-surgical complications.

Scalp reductions. A scalp reduction involves the surgical removal of a portion of the balding area. Once the excess skin has been removed, sutures are sewn in, pulling the remaining scalp tissue together, reducing the overall surface area of the scalp and "shrinking" your bald spot. Scalp reductions are recommended for hair thinning at the hairline, as opposed to the "doughnut" some men develop on their crowns. The procedure is often followed by mini-graft surgeries to fill in the remaining balding areas.

The hair "lift." For men whose receding hairlines have progressed far enough so that they have little or no hair on top of their heads, surgical lifts may be recommended. In this procedure, the whole scalp is moved up and forward during a two to three hour operation. Surgical lifts are high-priced and hard core: a large portion of your hair and scalp are removed from the area behind the temples and then re-planted on the front part of your head to create a new hairline.

Beyond the initial costs of consultation and surgery, SharpMen should expect to incur additional expenses for "maintaining" their new looks, including additional consultations, haircuts, dyes and replacements.

SHARPNOTE ON BALD IS BEAUTIFUL: Deciding whether to replace hair — by way of implants or otherwise — is a personal decision. Ultimately, the way *you* view your hair is far more important than the opinion of the women you meet. After all, there are always going to be those women who claim that they are not attracted to men with thinning hair. Of course, there are also many women who claim that they are not attracted to men who are not blonde and blue-eyed.

The point is — who cares?

It's impossible to appeal to all women everywhere, and there is some merit to presenting yourself as you are. If you feel comfortable with the way your hair looks, you're bound to be much more appealing to women than if you go out and spend money on a hair transplant process that may end up looking — well — *bad*.

In other words, *project confidence and the women will respond.* As for those women who can't see past your hairline — who wants them, anyway?

THE GROOMING ISSUE:

THINNING HAIR & COMB-OVERS

THE FACTS:

While they may sound like a great alternative to treatment shampoos and surgery, combing hair from the side of your head over a receding

REQUIRED GEAR

• Comb or brush.

hairline can do more harm than good. Alternatively, the right haircut, style and attitude can go a long way towards highlighting the hair you *do* have.

THE GROOMING SOLUTION:

To cut and style your hair in a way that makes it look thicker, ask your stylist to trim your hair shorter than he or she normally would – approximately one inch from your scalp, so that your hair does not create a "part." Shorten hair in stages to avoid going too short and looking like Caesar. To style, comb your hair down on the back and sides and forward on top. The short length and *forward* comb will look much more natural than a side comb-over, in addition to maximizing on the volume of your thin hair.

THE GROOMING ISSUE:
Thinning Hair on a Windy Day

THE FACTS:

For some SharpMen, the idea of going out onto a windy beach sounds pretty bad. Many guys are sensitive about a hairline that may have

> # REQUIRED GEAR
>
> • Cargo or baseball cap.

receded over the winter months. Other guys have hairstyles that require brushing the hair they *do* have over a bare doughnut. None of these guys have hair that cooperates on a windy day.

THE GROOMING SOLUTION:

Cap it. One obvious option is to wear a hat. Hats take your mind off the look of your hair and in addition to protecting the skin on your head from the sun. When choosing a hat for your beach or windy day activity, choose a cargo or baseball cap that fits well enough not to blow off, but not so tight that your scalp can't breathe — recently determined to be a contributing factor to hair loss. Cotton or mesh fabrics fit well, breathe well and easily absorb perspiration.

Snip it. Altering your hairstyle for outdoor activities and beach weather is an option many SharpMen fail to consider. In fact, it's common for men to opt for an "active" hairstyle or length when needed. Why not reshape your hair for summer, choosing a style that is conducive to a more active outdoor schedule?

Hairstylists who specialize in styling thinning hair often recommend shorter summer cuts for this reason. Shorter hair has a tendency to look fuller and is less affected by high winds. Too nervous to play with your existing cut? Discuss this option with your stylist the next time you go in for a trim. He or she will likely have a photo of the recommended style.

THE GROOMING ISSUE: GRAYING HAIR

THE FACTS:

Early graying is common among SharpMen, although eventually, nearly all SharpMen's hair will turn gray. The effect of "premature" graying? A more "seasoned" look on the job – a boost with many managers and clients. As for the ladies, the good news is that women don't seem to mind a change in seasons. And for those women looking for a "stable" guy, your new gray look may serve as the perfect prop.

THE GROOMING SOLUTION:

If you decide the gray is not for you, or prefer less gray, there's nothing wrong with a little color. Don't worry about vanity. After all, is getting a great-looking haircut vain? How about a flattering suit? Maybe, but who cares? It's not like you have to advertise your grooming regimen, anyway.

To avoid messing with at-home kits, ask your hairdresser to wash in a color rinse the next time you get a trim. *It's that easy.*

Another option: "fade" your gray using one of the many gradual color treatments. These products – either professional treatments or home shampoos – work over time, making your transition less obvious. Ask your hairstylist for a recommendation.

SHARPNOTE: If you choose to cover your gray, make a point of maintaining it every time you go in for a trim to avoid having your "roots show."

SHARPHANDS AND FEET
Hands & Fingernail Care
Nail Chewing
Ugly Feet
Toenail Care
Athlete's Foot
Dry, Cracked Heels
Corns & Calluses

YOUR BEST SIDE: THE SHARPBACK
Posture
Hair Removal
Back Acne

THOSE LITTLE PROBLEMS
Moles & Skin Tags
Safe Tanning
Surgical Body Sculpting
Tattoo Removal

THE GROOMING ISSUE:
SHARP HANDS & FINGERNAIL CARE

THE FACTS:

Sorry, buddy: women *do* notice your hands. And while the rugged look is considered attractive, the beauty of dirty fingernails seems to be lost on the women-folk *and* that place where you pick up a paycheck.

Then there's the rough hand issue. Sure calluses are a man's way of proving his gender, but touching women's skin with those sand-paper covered numbers is another complaint department altogether. With a few simple tips, it *is* possible to strike a balance between maintaining your guy-style hands and a hand shake that doesn't leave a scar.

> ## REQUIRED GEAR
>
> ───◆───
>
> • Light moisturizing hand cream.
> • Nail clippers or scissors.

THE GROOMING SOLUTION:

Hand cleaning for nails. The best thing you can do for your nails is to keep your *hands* clean. Make a point of washing your hands after work and after dirt-magnet activities. Work your forefinger and thumbnails under the opposing nails to pick out dirt.

Hand lube. A little *too* into that hand-washing routine? You may find that frequent hand washing — particularly if you use harsh "antibacterial" soaps — can cause your hands and fingernails to become dry and scaly. To avoid this, get yourself a light moisturizing hand cream, available at your local drugstore or in your medicine cabinet from two girlfriends ago.

Nail trimming. Another easy way to keep hands and nails looking clean and professional is to simply trim your nails more often than you currently do. Keeping your nails short will prevent pockets of dirt from accumulating under your nails. For trimming, avoid using the clippers you use on your toes. Toenail clippers tend to break nails, leaving you with jagged nail pieces. Since you *clearly* don't intend to *file* down those nubs of yours, use the right tool for the job. Consider investing in a pair of scissors or clippers made especially for trimming fingernails.

Cuticle patrol. Once you've trimmed your nails, take a moment to push back your cuticles — you know, those crusty boundaries of skin at the base of your nails. As your nails grow, the cuticle skin builds up and may develop a big "hump" of dead skin. After a while it may tear and bleed. Simply pushing these guys back before the geyser of blood erupts can make a big difference in how your nails look to others. To push back cuticles, simply use your opposing thumbnail to gently plow back the pieces of skin still hanging onto your nail. It's best to do this once a week or so, after you shower, when your skin is most pliable. As with anything, resist the urge to be too aggressive, or bacteria will take up residence at the base of your nail.

THE GROOMING ISSUE: FINGERNAIL BITERS

THE FACTS:

In this germ-conscious world, no one wants to shake hands with a guy who's just pulled his fingers out of his mouth. Despite this, fingernail-biting is surprisingly common among adult SharpMen.

It's an easy habit to form but a tough one to stop. For many men, nail-biting is so well-established that they barely realize how often they do it.

If you're ready to kick the habit, it's helpful to isolate your reasons for biting your nails in the first place:

REQUIRED GEAR

• Nail clippers.
• Bad-tasting formula.
• Stress ball, pad of paper or desktop game.
• Gum or mints.

Old habit. Many SharpMen can trace their nail-chomping back to their shy and self-conscious teenage years. Now they do it without thinking.

Stress. Tension is one of the leading reasons people begin — and continue — to bite their nails. Biting and picking become automatic reactions to the stress of a challenging job or a worrisome dilemma.

Nerves. Nail-biting can have the same soothing psychological effect as smoking or overeating. It's not uncommon to resort to nail-biting when you're feeling nervous before a big meeting or date.

Post-smoking habit. Those who give up smoking often replace their habit with nail-biting — it's something to do with hands that would have been occupied by a cigarette.

Habit triggered by another activity. Often nail-biting is associated with an activity such as talking on the phone or watching television. Some people bite their nails when bored or unoccupied (e.g. sitting on the train or in the doctor's office).

THE GROOMING SOLUTION:

By isolating your reasons for biting your nails — and then briefly monitoring yourself under the same conditions — you'll be more likely to stop your hands from automatically going to your mouth. If willpower isn't enough, consider the following remedies:

Put a formula on your nails. Visit your local drugstore for one of several foul-tasting formulas aimed at making your nails taste bad enough to turn you off of biting them — or at least alert you to when you do it unconsciously. Apply the colorless product to your fingernails and make a point of reapplying regularly to ensure that the foul taste remains strong.

Keep your hands busy. Idle hands are likely to fuel your habit, so keep them busy. If you've found that you bite your nails when you are on the telephone, keep a pad of paper and pen handy for doodling. Alternatively, invest in a desktop game to keep your hands busy or play solitaire on your desktop computer.

If you bite your nails when you're tense, consider adding a "stress ball" to your collection of desk toys. The key is to do anything that keeps your hands busy and out of your mouth.

Chew gum or mints. Seasoned nail-biters know that nail pieces and chewing gum are a bad combo. The next time you catch yourself chomping at your own body parts, pop a stick of gum or mint into your mouth.

Use nail clippers. Always tempted to bite off a sharp nail edge or "even out" a nail that is a little longer than the others? Avoid these excuses by trimming your nails regularly and keeping a pair of nail clippers in your desk or gym bag.

Make nail care a priority. Now that you've stopped biting your nails, take a few minutes to learn how to take care of them. See the *Sharp Hand and Fingernail Care* section of this guidebook for more information. By spending a bit of effort to get your hands in handshake-ready form, you'll be less likely to "fall off the wagon" and return to nail-biting.

THE GROOMING ISSUE: UGLY FEET

THE FACTS:

Ever go to the beach? Ugly feet can distract women from your better attributes.

THE GROOMING SOLUTION:

To solve the majority of unsightly foot problems, consider adding the following to your weekly grooming regimen:

Wash feet daily in *warm*, soapy water. Never soak your feet for more than ten minutes. Over-soaking can weaken the nails, which leads to breaking and chipping and, well, *ugly feet.*

> ### REQUIRED GEAR
>
> —•◦•—
>
> • Moisturizing lotion.
> • Fresh socks for every day between laundry days.
> • An alternate pair of canvas or leather shoes that fit well.

Dry feet thoroughly after every wash, especially between the toes where smelly fungus feels most comfortable growing and your skin tends to become dry and cracked.

Lube feet. If the skin on your feet is dry and scaly, apply a moisturizing product. To prevent fungal growth, avoid applying moisturizer between your toes.

Change socks daily. Stock up on socks that allow your feet to breathe.

Wear shoes that fit. Tight-fitting shoes can contribute to the development of ingrown toenails – major players in the ugly feet phenomenon.

Alternate shoes that breathe. When choosing your "everyday" shoes, opt for breathable, natural materials, such as canvas or leather. This is particularly important if your feet are prone to sweating. When removing your shoes at night, avoid stuffing your socks back into the shoes — give the interior a chance to air out. Alternate your "everyday" shoes every couple of days to ensure that they dry out completely.

THE GROOMING ISSUE:

TOENAIL CARE & INGROWN TOENAILS

THE FACTS:

Even if you're not a sandals kind of guy, keeping your toenails trimmed properly will prevent ingrown toenails, a condition where poorly trimmed nails grow into the skin. Ingrown toenails are painful. They inhibit your ability to walk and wear shoes

> ## REQUIRED GEAR
>
> • Toenail clippers.
> • Shoes that do not pinch at the toes.

comfortably. Once they develop, the condition is best treated by a podiatrist, a doctor specializing in the care of feet. Simply trimming your toenails properly can prevent this painful foot ailment.

THE GROOMING SOLUTION:

The most important part of toenail care is simple: use clippers made for *toes*. Because fingernail clippers are not wide enough to cut straight across the toe, they force you to round out toenails as you trim – a big mistake. Improper cutting is a major cause of ingrown toenails.

On the other hand, clippers designed for use on toenails are wide enough to trim your toenail in one stroke – straight across – leaving the edges of your toenails above the skin on either side. When trimming, make a point of cutting straight from end to end, as rounding out the sides will make it more likely that your shoes will push your skin over the toenail and cause the sides of the nail to grow into your skin. Ouch. The best news? Toenail clippers are cheap; another good reason to get the right tool for the job.

Purchasing shoes that fit properly is another easy way to avoid ingrown toenails. Pass on any shoe that pinches at the toes.

THE GROOMING ISSUE:
COMBATING ATHLETE'S FOOT

THE FACTS:

Ever have an itch on your foot that makes you want to shove your leg into the freezer? Ever try it? Before compromising the ecosystems of major household appliances, check out the facts about athlete's foot and what you can do to get it under control.

Athlete's foot is caused by a fungus that grows in moist, warm areas. The condition is generally associated with peeling skin or areas of redness on the feet. Some people also suffer from uncontrollable itching and a *really* unpleasant foot odor. The bottom line? If you have this condition, your feet look *bad*.

REQUIRED GEAR

- Shoetrees.
- Fresh socks for every day between laundry days.
- An alternate pair of canvas or leather shoes that fit well.
- Pool or shower shoes.
- Foot powder or spray.

If your feet are prone to sweating or spend the majority of the day in dress shoes or athletic shoes, you've probably already battled this condition.

THE GROOMING SOLUTION:

The best way to control athlete's foot is to avoid the circumstances under which it develops.

Change. A chief cause of athlete's foot is remnant moisture in the inner leather lining of your shoes. That's right; sometimes the fungus develops *in your shoes.* Make a point of changing shoes as often as practical, giving each pair a chance to dry.

Choose. If your feet spend the majority of their days in shoes, choose shoes made of leather or canvas – materials that allow feet to breathe.

Air dry. When you take off your shoes, don't stuff your socks back into them – this prevents your shoes from airing out properly and creates a nice, moist environment for the growth of fungus. Instead, place your shoes in a well-ventilated area between use.

- *For dress shoes,* purchase and use cedar shoetrees. Quality shoetrees help absorb moisture and sustain the shape of your dress shoes.

- *For athletic shoes,* loosen the shoelaces and pull the tongues out, thereby exposing the interior to light and air.

Change again. Avoid wearing the same socks two days in a row. If you have a chance to do so, switch to a dry pair of socks between your day and evening activities. When stocking up on socks, choose socks made from fabrics that wick moisture away from the foot; acrylic is particularly good for this purpose.

Sprinkle or spray. If your feet are prone to sweating, visit your drugstore for foot powder or foot powder spray. Sprinkle or spray the powder on your feet and into your socks to cut down on the moisture caused by sweating.

Wash. When you wash your feet, make a point of cleaning between the toes with soap and water. Then thoroughly dry your feet, particularly in between your toes.

Wear sandals or flip-flops in locker rooms at the gym and around the pool to protect your feet from other guys' fungi. That's right; *the fungus you carry may not be your own…*

If you suspect that you've developed athlete's foot, see a podiatrist who can prescribe anti-fungal medication to control the fungus and the itching. In extreme circumstances, your doctor may recommend nail surgery.

THE GROOMING ISSUE: DRY, CRACKED HEELS

THE FACTS:

Dry, cracked heels are a big problem for lots of guys. Unlike women, many SharpMen are less likely to moisturize when they get out of the shower. In winter or during seasons when bare feet and open-toe shoes are in and out of water, the skin on the

REQUIRED GEAR

• Gentle, non-drying soap.
• Antibacterial ointment.
• Petroleum jelly.
• Gym socks.

bottom of your feet can dry out. The result? A painful cracking of the skin on the bottoms of your feet and possible infection.

THE GROOMING SOLUTION:

The following tips will help soothe and heal dry, cracked heels:

Step One: Clean. Your first job is to ensure that the cracked areas of your skin – basically exposed wounds – do not become infected. Wash your feet thoroughly before you turn in at night. Use a gentle soap less likely to further irritate your skin.

Step Two: Disinfect. Apply an over-the-counter antibacterial ointment to the cracked areas. Use a lot.

Step Three: Lube up. After applying the ointment, take half of a golf ball-sized amount of a petroleum jelly, and slather it all over your feet — particularly on the area where your heels are cracked.

Step Four: Cover up. Once your feet are well-lubed, slowly put a gym sock over each foot, being careful not to wipe off too much of the jelly and ointment.

Step Five: Go to sleep. In the morning, remove the gym socks and wipe off any excess jelly that did not absorb. If possible, remain barefoot for a while to give the open wounds time to dry out.

Step Six: Reapply. When you get out of the shower, take a *small* amount of petroleum jelly and rub it on the dry part of your heel before putting on your shoes. Wash, dry and repeat this small application when you get home from work, but this time leave your shoes off to let your heels breathe.

Step Seven: Repeat the sock routine for about a week or until your heels start looking better. You may want to do this more often during winter and other drying times of the year.

Step Eight: Keep an eye on things. If you notice your cracked heels getting worse or looking red and inflamed, see a physician. You may be allergic to one of the products used. Your doctor will check for infection and give you something for your heels that does not contain the chemical agent you are reacting to.

THE GROOMING ISSUE: CORNS & CALLUSES

THE FACTS:

Guys who do a lot of walking
or engage in athletic activities
often have feet riddled with
corns and calluses — great
for walking on glass, bad for
your feet.

Corns and calluses are caused
by a thickening of the skin,
which builds up in layers on the toes (corns) and heels (calluses) of
your feet. This build-up can cause dress shoes to pinch and
become less comfortable.

REQUIRED GEAR

• Shoes that fit the shape of
  your foot.
• Thongs or sandals.
• Corn or callus remover.

THE GROOMING SOLUTION:

If you're self-conscious about the build-up of skin on your
feet, consider:

Your shoes. Like blisters, corns and calluses are often caused by
ill-fitting shoes that rub against the skin on your feet. Make a point
of choosing shoes that fit the shape of your foot.

Your habits. Walking barefoot is another cause of corns and
calluses. Consider throwing on a pair of thongs or sandals the next
time you're planning a stroll.

Removal. If removal of corns and calluses is your plan, you'll find
a variety of no-pain and no-brainer remedies sold over-the-counter
at your local drugstore. Most require a one-time application.

They're back. If your corns and calluses persist, you may have a
problem that cannot be remedied at home. For example, you may
walk or position your foot in a way that promotes the growth of
corns and calluses. Visit a podiatrist, a doctor specializing in foot
care, for an "orthotic" insert, a device worn in your shoes that
corrects foot position and abnormal foot motion.

THE GROOMING ISSUE:
IMPROVING YOUR POSTURE

THE FACTS:

The most obvious drawback to poor posture is a slumped look that conveys a lack of confidence. Internally there can be other, more serious problems. Standing, walking or sitting incorrectly can cause muscle tension, unnatural

> ### REQUIRED GEAR
> ————•◦•————
> • Several small pillows.
> • Back support cushion.

strain on ligaments and joints, improperly aligned bones, headaches, fatigue, shoulder, neck and back pain and other adverse effects on the position and function of your internal organs.

How's your posture?

What looks fine to you may look like a "walking question mark" to others. To determine whether your posture could use some home improvement, ask a friend or doctor to watch the way you walk, sit and stand. Alternatively, study your reflection as you walk past a storefront. Are your shoulders slumped forward? Is your head down? Or do you hold your back stiff and your head thrown forward? If the answer is yes to any of these questions, your body would benefit from a posture revamping.

THE GROOMING SOLUTION:

Sleep correctly. Avoid sleeping on your stomach. Instead, aim to sleep on your back or on your side. If you prefer to sleep on your back, place a pillow under your head and shoulders, another rolled pillow or "neck roll" under your neck, and a third pillow under your knees. This position will provide maximum support to your spine. For SharpMen who sleep on their side, place a pillow under your head, making sure that your neck is supported and that your head is level with your spine. Place a second pillow between your bent knees. If you find that you tend to roll forward once you nod off, place a third pillow in front of your chest.

Lift with your knees. When lifting objects, bend at the knees and use your leg and stomach muscles to lift, rather than your back. If you find that you can't help but lift with your back, consider getting a weight belt for the gym and other lifting activities.

Carry close to your chest. When carrying heavy items, try to hold them close to your chest. This simple change will take some of the strain from your shoulders and back and help improve your posture.

Stand with one foot raised. If you must stand for a sustained amount of time, place one foot on a chair or stool, changing feet often. If you can't use a footstool, occasionally shift your weight between your feet, bending slightly at the knees and keeping your spine straight.

Support your lower back while seated. When sitting for long periods of time, place a rolled towel or cushion behind your lower back and push your rear into the back of the chair. Try to position your knees so that they are level with, or slightly above, your hips with your feet flat on the floor.

Adjust your driving seat. While driving, position your seat close enough to the wheel and pedals to avoid leaning in. Position the headrest to support the middle of your head and sit with your back firmly against the seat.

Walk straight. When walking, try to keep your head up and eyes straight ahead. Hold your shoulders back, but not to the point where the position requires you to tense up or push your head forward.

Stretch regularly. If you must sit for long periods of time, take a break and walk around every hour or so. If strolling is not an option, try stretching in your seat. For example, look up, raise your arms over your head, inhale deeply and hold this position for 10 seconds. Repeat six times. Alternatively, slowly roll your head clockwise three times and then counterclockwise three times.

Get regular exercise and eat properly. Overall good health always helps to maintain your body's top form. Activities like cycling or swimming are particularly beneficial for strengthening your back and improving your posture. Eating fresh fruits and vegetables, drinking eight glasses of water per day and recharging your body with regular sleep intervals will help fight fatigue and dehydration – two factors that contribute to poor posture.

THE GROOMING ISSUE: REMOVING BACK HAIR

THE FACTS:

Some SharpMen have hairy backs; other SharpMen don't. The "right" look is a matter of personal preference. For those guys who prefer less back hair for summer activities, temporary and permanent hair removal options abound.

THE GROOMING SOLUTION:

Shaving. Although shaving is by far your least expensive option, it is also the least permanent. Nonetheless, for guys who need a quick fix, shaving may be your best bet.

Will shaving body hair make it grow back thicker? No—that's a myth. Neither shaving, trimming or cutting head or body hair makes hair grow any faster or thicker. So go for it.

Regardless of whether you use an electric or traditional

REQUIRED GEAR

For shaving:
- Razor.
- Light moisturizing balm.
- Someone to shave you.

razor, one basic rule applies: *don't shave yourself.* Shaving a hard-to-reach area like your back can spell disaster. Not only will you miss large spots of hair, you'll be more likely to injure yourself in the process. Ask your SharpWoman or your buddy to help out.

Once you're set up, hop into the shower. The heat and water will open up your pores and soften your skin and back hairs, making it easier for you to shave and harder for you to cut yourself. Softening skin will also help prevent razor burn and other inflammations.

If you plan to use a traditional razor, ask your assistant to apply a thick layer of shaving cream to the designated shaving area. This is an easy way to control just how far up your shoulders and down your back your assistant will shave – *before* it's too late. Ask your helper to use short strokes down your back rather than shaving against the grain of hair growth. Remind him or her to rinse the razor in hot water every five strokes to prevent snags and cuts.

Once the electric razor is off or the shaving cream is gone, finish off your shave by applying a light moisturizer to prevent the razor burn and breakouts that often result from post-shave dryness and irritation.

Waxing. Another great short-term hair removal method is waxing. Unlike shaving, which only lasts about three days, most men only need to wax their backs once a month.

Often used by athletes, waxing is performed in a private room at a salon or spa. The basic method goes like this: a licensed aesthetician (what used to be called a "beautician") warms a pot of wax and uses a large tongue depressor to spread the wax onto your back. He or she places a small piece of cloth onto the wax-covered area. The cloth and wax combination is then quickly removed — taking your hair and roots with it. Although this might seem painful — and it can be — the pain only lasts about thirty seconds, and is a small price to pay for hair-free skin.

One problem associated with waxing is the possibility of a post-wax acne breakout or rash. To prevent this, most attendants use a pre-wax treatment, like a powder. After the treatment, the aesthetician may apply alcohol to remove the wax and disinfect. Taking a shower directly after a waxing also helps reduce the possibility of breakouts and redness.

Laser treatments. Laser hair removal uses an invisible beam of light to permanently disable the growth of hair follicles. Of course, nothing is magic. The small laser-directing tip treats only dime-sized to one-inch areas per "shot." Consequently, you may require a few hours per treatment and several return visits to treat your entire back. Laser back hair removal can be uncomfortable and tends to be more expensive than other treatments.

Electrolysis. Electrolysis treatments target individual hairs, burning the root of the hair follicle in order to permanently retard regrowth. The upside? You can remove your back hair forever. The downside? It's painful and, like laser hair removal, the electrolysis process can last up to a year, depending on the amount of hair on your back.

Why so long? Every square inch of our bodies has the potential to produce 5,000 hair follicles. Because electrolysis must target the root of *each* individual follicle in order to permanently remove it, an average electrolysis treatment can require a lot of your time — on average, about an hour once a week for a year. Many treatment facilities offer late-night hours to accommodate busy SharpMen.

SHARPNOTE: Are you prone to back acne? If so, waxing can further irritate this sensitive condition. Consider waiting until your back clears up before using a waxing treatment to remove back hair.

THE GROOMING ISSUE: PREVENTING BACK ACNE

THE FACTS:

Never get to play the "skins" team in B-ball? Always feel like all eyes are on your back in the locker room? Treat your back acne and both concerns will fade away.

THE GROOMING SOLUTION:

Choose right. You may not realize it, but like other parts of your body, your back has *a lot* of oil glands. But unlike your face or, in some cases, your arms, your back is covered up all day. If you wear breathable cotton undershirts to keep sweat from staining your clothes, your cotton Ts may be contributing to your

> ### REQUIRED GEAR
>
> - Loofah scrubber with a long handle.
> - Acne medication.
> - Non-absorbent undershirts.
> - Oil-free sunscreen.

back acne. Because cotton is so absorbent, it holds sweat in the fabric – and close to your skin – all day. If you find that you have problems with back acne, consider switching to synthetic undershirts that wick moisture away from your skin. Similarly, after workouts, change out of sweaty cotton gym clothes as soon as practical.

Change right. Make a point of wearing a clean shirt or undershirt every day – even if it's had time to "breathe" overnight, a shirt that has absorbed back skin oils is more likely to cause back acne.

Wash right. Ready to hit the shower? Visit your local drugstore for a long-handled "loofah" sponge or other abrasive scrubbing aid to remove dead skin cells while you soap up. Dead skin cells clog up pores and lead to breakouts. The more often you remove these dead skin cells the better off your back will be.

With your loofah in hand, lather up and scrub away. The idea is to *gently* remove excess cells; apply enough pressure to do the job, but not so much as to cause redness or skin irritation. For those SharpMen who feel that their backs need extra help, consider using a cleanser designed especially for body acne.

Dry right. Use a fresh towel to dry your back thoroughly. Covering open pores on a damp back is an invitation to acne and skin irritation.

Treat right. You can also spot treat your back acne with a topical gel or lotion. Keep in mind that, because back acne is cooped up in your sweaty clothes all day, it may be slower to respond than the kind you use on your face. For this reason, only apply the medication where you actually have acne. Otherwise, you'll end up drying out your back and creating red and itchy areas.

Hairy considerations. Do you have long head hair? If your mane hangs against your skin or creates a small sweat bath when it's against your cotton shirt, your locks may be aggravating the pores on your back. Consider washing your hair more often to prevent oil build-up, giving it a trim or wearing it up and away from your back.

Sun treatments. Many SharpMen who suffer from winter back breakouts look forward to summer — when baring their back to the sun seems to temporarily clear up their acne problem. But beware: beyond the increased risk of skin cancer, blasts of sun exposure may clear up your back at the expense of scarring sensitive zit-covered skin. Then, come winter, your back may look worse than ever.

Use sunscreen when exposing your back — or any other part of our skin — to the sun. Worried that goopy sunscreen will promote more breakouts? Pick up an oil-free sunscreen that protects your skin from sun, scarring and zits.

SHARPNOTE: Most over-the-counter acne medications contain *benzoyl peroxide*. This effective acne-fighting ingredient may bleach your clothing if you don't allow the medication to fully absorb and dry prior to putting on your clothes.

THE GROOMING ISSUE: MOLES & SKIN TAGS

THE FACTS:

In a world where clear skin is hip, many SharpMen feel that that their moles and skin tags are not. And while these skin marks are normal, they demand some attention and care.

Moles and skin tags are non-malignant (non-cancerous) skin growths that tend to be inherited. Almost everyone has a few moles; most people have between ten and forty throughout their body. They usually appear in childhood or adolescence and continue to develop into a SharpMan's forties. Moles can be small or large; flesh-colored, yellow-brown, or black; flat or raised; smooth, hairy or wart-like. Many moles begin as small, flat spots and slowly become raised and grow larger in diameter. The majority are round or oval, no bigger than a pencil eraser. Over many years, moles may flatten again, become flesh-colored, or even disappear.

In the same family of moles are skin tags; soft, small, flesh-colored or other-colored growths, usually occurring in multiples on the neck, eyelids, armpits and groin. Skin tags are generally harmless but may be irritating, especially if they catch on clothing or rub against your collar.

Years ago, studies erroneously linked skin tags with colon cancer. Since then, researchers have found that simply gaining weight can increase the development of skin tags.

THE GROOMING SOLUTION:

Care for moles and skin tags. While most are harmless, some moles can cause considerable health problems. For this reason it is necessary to properly care for and monitor your moles. For example:

- Moles that suddenly change in color or size should be evaluated by a physician to ensure that the change does not indicate melanoma, a serious form of skin cancer.

Other warning signs include itching, crusting, pain and bleeding.

- Exposing moles to the sun increases the usual risk of skin cancer. Keep your moles covered and out of the sun.
- Don't pick at your moles. If a mole is irritating you, speak to a dermatologist about having it removed.
- By contrast, skin tags are fairly harmless, rarely "changing" into something that requires medical attention or treatment.

Removal of moles. While the majority of moles do not *require* removal, they are often removed for cosmetic reasons. Your physician can remove moles by excision, liquid nitrogen, or banding, although most people choose to have their moles removed by a plastic surgeon or dermatologist to minimize scarring.

Moles that have developed on the surface of the skin can also be shaved off by a doctor in a "shave biopsy." The area around the mole is numbed with local anesthesia and the mole is shaved off. This procedure does not generally produce scarring, however, in some cases a whitish discoloration remains.

Moles that grow deeper, into the second layer of the skin, require a "punch biopsy," wherein local anesthesia is applied and a small, cookie cutter-like device is used to remove the mole. As a precautionary measure, each mole removed is sent to a laboratory to ensure that it's non-cancerous.

Removal of skin tags. By contrast, removal of skin tags is less involved and is often performed by a general physician. Methods include freezing the tag with liquid nitrogen, tying off the tag with a thread or suture to cut off the blood supply, or cutting off the tag with a scalpel or scissors – all with minimal patient discomfort.

SHARPNOTE: Health insurance coverage for mole and skin tag removal varies, so check with your health plan before having the procedure performed. If you do have a biopsy, consider forking out a bit more to have a d*ermapathologist,* a doctor with specific training in interpreting skin biopsies, review your results.

THE GROOMING ISSUE: SAFE TANNING

THE FACTS:

Sure you don't want skin cancer, but is the price of healthy skin a blinding white torso? Not at all. Rather than spending time and money on a trip to the sunny side of the street, many

> ### REQUIRED GEAR
>
> • Tanning cream, spray or accelerator.
> • Sunscreen SPF 15 or higher.

SharpMen are discovering a faster, safer and less expensive option: *self-tanning products* – grooming aids that safely change the color of your skin from white to golden.

In the past, tanning creams were tricky: most turned skin orange, rather than golden brown, and if not applied evenly, they produced a "splotchy" effect. Today's re-engineered, easier-to-use products have given tanning creams a better name.

THE GROOMING SOLUTION:

If you'd like to use a tanning cream or spray, consider the following tips for best results:

Clean. Begin with clean, dry skin.

Apply a light coat of the cream or spray on your skin. Use less than you think you need.

Blend the cream or spray quickly and evenly on your skin.

When applying to the face, first apply the product to your hands, rub your hands together to spread the product and then blend evenly onto the face. Avoid direct contact with the eye area; the skin around the eyes is generally lighter in color than other facial skin, so this will actually look more natural.

Stop. You may not notice an immediate color change after your initial application, but resist the temptation to apply more. Your new color will become obvious in two to four hours.

Wash hands in hot soapy water immediately after using the product.

Wait to put on your clothing until the tanning lotion has dried completely. Avoid swimming and bathing for an hour after your application.

By giving yourself a nice "base" coat of color, you'll be less self-conscious about hitting the water and less likely to fry your skin. If you'd like to slowly transition your faux color to a safe tan, generously apply sunscreen whenever you expose your skin to the sun and your color-from-a-bottle will slowly transition into a long-lasting summer tan.

THE GROOMING ISSUE: Surgical Body Sculpting Options for Guys

THE FACTS:

Wish you had perfect abs or pecs? Can't seem to lose those love handles? While altering one's outward appearance — especially surgically — is by no means required to be a true SharpMan, those guys who *are* curious about doing so are no less sharp. After all, if it makes you feel better, why not?

And, frankly, you wouldn't be alone. Plastic surgery is becoming more and more common among men.

THE GROOMING SOLUTION:

For information on facial cosmetic surgery options, see the *Facial Cosmetic Surgery for Guys* section of this guidebook. Common *below-the-neck* procedures for guys include:

Liposuction. This is the one for those love handles. Guys also turn to liposuction for *gynecomastia,* a condition where fat accumulates around the breast area, preventing pectoral muscles from responding to workouts. Liposuction is also used to remove second chins and that area around your abdomen that seems to grow wider each year you keep your desk job.

Plastic surgeons advise all candidates to try diet and exercise before opting to go under the knife. Otherwise, the fat you have sucked out may come right back in other areas. Other complications include an accumulation of fluid, prolonged swelling and temporary loss of sensation in the area where your surgery was performed.

Muscle enhancement. Calf implants, pectoral implants and abdominal etching are common among men looking to surgically enhance their muscle definition. Muscle etching is a type of liposuction that creates a more defined look in the abdominal area. Calf and pectoral implants are what they sound like — implants designed to make your muscle formation look more pronounced, without the associated workouts. The procedure for pectoral implants is very similar to a breast augmentation for women. A small incision is made in the armpit and implants are placed under the muscle, giving the appearance of bulkier muscles.

With calf implants, it may take up to a week before you can walk normally. Possible complications with the implants include irregular shape after the swelling goes down and loss of sensation in the areas where the surgery was performed.

Penile enhancement. In a penile enhancement procedure, surgeons remove fat from one part of the body (such as your love handles) and inject it into the penis to increase penile length. The actual lengthening occurs after the procedure, when the patient is required to wear a weight attached to his penis – the weight stretches out the ligament that connects the penis to the pubic bone.

To add to penile girth (making it thicker), your doctor will use something called *AlloDerm*™, a substance made from human skin. Some risks of this procedure include scarring in the area, infection and some measure of deformity.

Cost. Surgical procedures of this type can cost anywhere from a few hundred dollars for an in-office procedure to several thousand dollars for more complicated ones. Because most procedures are considered elective, they may not be covered by your insurance. As you run the numbers, factor in the added costs of recovery time away from the office and your social life.

To find out more about a variety of the procedures available to men, contact a local dermatologist or plastic surgery specialist.

THE GROOMING ISSUE: TATTOO REMOVAL

THE FACTS:

Many SharpMen look at their arms and wonder, "What was I thinking? I don't even know this girl anymore…" For those who consider removing their tattoos prior to a golf weekend with the boss, tattoo removal can help erase what you no longer remember.

In the past, techniques for removing tattoos were pretty harsh. Whether *dermabrasion, salabrasion, Argon* or *CO_2 lasers* were used, red, blue and black ink could not be removed successfully, and the patient was often left with unsightly scar tissue. Today, new laser treatments yield much better results with red, blue and black inks and significantly reduce the formation of scar tissue. Treatments are usually administered by dermatologists and other physicians certified in laser treatment.

THE GROOMING SOLUTION:

Sun power. Just as excessive sun exposure can fade and dilute tattoo lines over time, the new types of tattoo removal treatments use the energy of light to break down and fade tattoo ink. The advantage is that new tattoo removal lasers do this much more quickly and safely. The lasers are designed to channel only one or two specific wavelengths of light in very short, powerful bursts, thereby breaking down tattoo inks and causing minimal damage to the skin, as compared to sun exposure or other tattoo removal methods. The wavelengths pass through the skin and break down tattoo ink so that it can be filtered out by the patient's body.

Success rates. It's hard for any procedure to work for all tattoos. Why? Over one hundred types of ink are used all over the world — *none* regulated by governmental agencies. More mysterious are the amounts and skin depths at which the inks are administered by various tattoo artists. For this reason, it is nearly impossible for physicians to predict how well a tattoo will fade before treatment. In most cases about ninety-five percent of the tattoo fades. Blue, black and red inks fade best; orange and purples next best; while green and yellow inks are the most difficult colors to remove.

Pain considerations. New treatments also make tattoo removal a lot less painful. The lasers used emit "pulses," or short bursts of light, that are felt for less than a second at a time. The feeling has been compared to a *very short* snap of a rubber band or a small amount of hot bacon grease on your arm — *but only for a second.* Only very sensitive SharpMen will require anesthesia, and then only locally.

After treatment, some SharpMen may experience pinpoint-sized bleeding in the immediate removal area, which will be cleaned and bandaged. You'll be able to shower the following day so long as you don't scrub the wound.

Treatment time. Does one shot do it? Not exactly. Removal of professional tattoos requires about five or six treatments, while amateur tattoos only require three or four sessions each spaced about a month apart. The number of sessions required depends on the amount and types of inks used and how deep they lie beneath the skin. Only the "worst" cases require ten visits or more.

SHARPNOTE: Got a corporate retreat coming up sooner than tattoo removal can deliver anonymity? Forget bandaging your arm – this will only call attention to what lies beneath. If your tattoo is on your arm, wear a T-shirt that comes down far enough to hide your ink and play on the "shirts" team. If questioned, answer honestly to avoid looking untrustworthy.

THE GROOMING ISSUE: USING COLOGNE WITHOUT GOING OVERBOARD

THE FACTS:

You want to smell good, but no man should smell *too* good.

Despite what cologne manufacturers would like you to believe, the best cologne application is a subtle one. Think of cologne in two ways: one, as insurance in case you reek; and two, as a special signature for those who come close enough to notice. In both cases, there's no need to go overboard. Just think *subtlety,* and your message will be just as strong.

THE GROOMING SOLUTION:

To manage your cologne application, consider the following:

Choose your tools. For those SharpMen who have a hard time regulating the amount of cologne they apply, stick with a spray product. Never exceed two pumps of the spray. If it is not possible to get a spray in your fragrance of choice, do what you can to avoid "splashing" like the actors in those aftershave commercials. After all, once the dam is open, volume can get out of control faster than you think.

Pick your application point. Certain areas of the body have a higher "burn rate" than others. These hot spots, frequently used by women, include the inner wrist, neck and other areas exposed to air. To keep these areas reeking all day, you'll have to start with a lot of scent in the morning — which often means that you arrive to work stinking like *Pepe Le Pew.* We don't recommend this.

Instead, apply a small amount to your hands and rub the cologne (or simply spray) to your *chest, back, thighs* or any other part of your body that is not exposed to air. This allows the scent of your cologne to emanate slowly and relatively evenly throughout the day. You'll also find that this technique ensures that you get more mileage out of expensive colognes.

SHARPNOTE: While it may be tempting, don't get carried away by the intimate possibilities of cologne. Avoid applying fragrance to your, uh, *organs,* or you'll be suffering from potentially painful consequences for a while. Impervious to pain? Then consider the fact that while it may smell sweet from two feet away, after marinating in your clothes up close and personal, your scent may be overpowering to the nose and bitter to the tongue. Enough said.

THE GROOMING ISSUE: CHOOSING COLOGNE

THE FACTS:

Tempted to save time and splash on any old scent you favor? Keep in mind that fragrances come in different concentration levels and scent families that are appropriate for various occasions and lifestyles. Sound complicated? Picking your signature scent is easier than you might think once you understand the basics.

THE GROOMING SOLUTION:

Choosing a concentration level. Fragrances come in varying levels of concentration, meaning some are stronger than others. For example, aftershave has the least amount of fragrance, *eau de toilette* has more, and *eau de cologne* contains even more. (*Eau de parfum* actually has the most, but this concentration is generally reserved for women's fragrances.) The higher the level of concentration you choose, the less cologne is required for a strong application.

Choosing a scent. Like descriptions of wine, a discussion of cologne scent characteristics can sound more like a botany lesson than an easy-to-understand guide to choosing a fragrance you like. To keep things simple, the following scents are divided into four categories: casual wear, daytime-office wear, evening wear, and romance wear:

Casual wear fragrances tend to be light, clean, crisp, and citrusy, and are appropriate for weekends, casual outings, college SharpMen, and less formal occupations. Look for scents that combine rosemary, lime, mandarin, iris, vanilla, musk, and cedar or mint, lavender, sandalwood, cedar and amber.

Daytime-office wear fragrances are generally refreshing, sharp and spicy and give off a "commanding" aura that is appropriate for professional environments when used in moderation. Look for fragrances that blend small amounts patchouli and sandalwood with woodsy undertones.

Evening wear. For guys who want to smell like they just left a power-meeting in order to "make an appearance" at a certain shindig, evening wear colognes are strong, exotic and refined. Look for fragrances that blend oak musk, lavender, grapefruit, and mandarin, lemon, orange, lavender, sage, cedar and believe it or not, tobacco.

Romantic scents are generally heavier and spicier, designed for more intimate occasions. Look for blends of cloves, jasmine, rose, coriander, vanilla, honey and even grass, or lemons, oranges and bergamot, combined with deeper notes of clove, coriander, nutmeg and aromatic wood. Studies indicate that the "right" scents can make women feel more romantically inclined. Hmmm...

Buying a scent. Ready to put your cash on the barrel? Take a small bag of coffee beans to your local department store and sniff around. Ask the salesperson to recommend scents that combine those ingredients that meet your fragrance needs (see above).

Ask for and spray the testers on small pieces of cardboard rather than your arms. Between each sniff, breathe into the coffee bean bag to "clean" your smell palette. Now try another. When you've narrowed your choices down to two or three, spray a small amount on different parts of your arms, make note of what you sprayed where and then walk away from the counter.

After about an hour, smell your skin again to see which scent you prefer. You'll find that the oils and the individual chemistry of your skin will change the way each cologne smells on you. Make your selection based on these "mature" scents.

THE GROOMING ISSUE: MAKING YOUR COLOGNE LAST

THE FACTS:

Maintaining a stockpile of cologne can be expensive. Of course, the longer you make it last, the less you will have to spend.

THE GROOMING SOLUTION:

To get more mileage out of the cologne you already own, consider the following:

Skin type. The length of time your cologne lasts is affected by your skin type. If you have oily skin, you're in luck: scent will last longer on you due to your skin's higher moisture content – potentially up to five or six hours. As such, go ahead and ease up on your applications.

SharpMen with dry skin will find that their colognes don't have quite as much stamina. Rather than applying more in the morning, consider dividing your morning routine by reapplying smaller amounts between activities.

Quality versus price. While low-cost knock-offs of popular colognes abound, the higher-quality ingredients and essential oils found in the real thing are likely to last several *hours* longer per application. Sure, you'll save a few bucks on the front end, but you'll also find yourself reapplying more often and depleting your supply much more quickly. Not much of a deal.

SHARPNOTE: Because cologne generally lasts only four to six hours, consider keeping an extra bottle in your desk drawer for a quick reapplication before you head out after work. Many types of cologne also come in trial and travel sizes perfect for this purpose. Of course, always remember that scents begin emanating the second you open the bottle. To avoid becoming the joke of your office (think "Tulip Boy"), remove yourself (and your bottle) to the men's room before uncorking and reapplying.

THE GROOMING ISSUE: STORING COLOGNE

THE FACTS:

Again, cologne is expensive. By simply using and storing it properly, you'll have to buy it less often. In fact, with proper storage and usage, high-quality cologne can last between five and seven years.

THE GROOMING SOLUTION:

To maximize the life of your cologne, consider the following:

Packaging. Colognes release their scent the moment you uncork them. The less often they are opened, the more powerful your fragrance will remain. Similarly, contaminants found on all hands – even freshly showered ones – weaken the scent of cologne. As such, spray colognes tend to last longer than splash colognes – you use less with every application and the fragrance does not come into contact your hands or the outside air due to the spray applicator.

Storage. According to fragrance experts, cologne should be stored in a manner similar to wine. Should you start constructing that cologne cellar in your basement? Not necessarily. Simply avoid exposing your colognes to heat, sunlight, and air. A bathroom cabinet or counter is fine, so long as the counter isn't exposed to direct sunlight. If possible, store the fragrance in its original box if you plan to wait awhile before using it.

THE GROOMING ISSUE:
SharpGrooming in the Locker Room

THE FACTS:

Due to heat in the showers, sauna, hot tub and steam room and the ever-present sweat and other bodily fluids, your gym's locker room becomes a haven for the growth of bacteria and germs.

> ## REQUIRED GEAR
>
> • Shower shoes or thongs.
> • Clean towel.
> • Clean socks.
> • Toiletry kit.

Do you walk around barefoot? If you do, you'll be a prime candidate for athlete's foot. Do you sit in the steam room and rest your back against the wall? If the guy before you had a skin rash, your chances of contracting it rise. Similarly, if the guy who shaved in the sink before you cut himself and failed to rinse the faucet, using the sink exposes you to infection. *Eeeeew.*

THE GROOMING SOLUTION:

Relax. Arming yourself against the unseen hazards of the locker room is as simple as following a few tips:

Cover your feet. Wear flip flops, sandals or water shoes. In addition to preventing slips and spills, simply wearing something to protect your feet provides a line of defense against other guys' athlete's foot and other infections.

Wash your towels. Many clubs provide clean towels. For those that require you to bring your own, make it a clean one. Don't let the same damp towel sit in your locker or gym bag week after week. Damp towels can quickly become breeding grounds for bacteria and germs, especially after you've hung them on the rack while showering – where other guys' sweaty towels were before. Ever seen a guy wiping down towel racks between customers? Neither have we. Make a point of swapping out your towels every few days.

Wear a towel or swim trunks while steaming. While the guy next to you may hit the sauna, steam room or hot tub in the buff, doctors recommend wearing swim trunks or sitting on and wrapping your lower body in a towel. This simply act of modesty protects you from lice and any bacteria present on the steam room seat. Wanna lean back against the tile? Consider putting a towel between the open pores on your back and the last guy who got cozy in the steam.

Change your socks. Bring a clean pair of socks to change into after your workout. Wearing the same pair of sweaty socks (particularly if they've picked up bacteria off the floor of the locker room) promotes the growth of athlete's foot.

Dry your back. A SharpMan's back is one of the hardest parts of the body to keep clean — and therefore the most vulnerable. Drying it thoroughly will help prevent the development of acne and help protect you from the spread of bacteria you may have picked up by leaning against the walls of steam rooms, tanning beds, saunas or hot tubs.

Separate toiletries. Always keep your toothbrush, soap and razor in a separate bag or container from the rest of your workout gear to avoid spreading bacteria from your clothing and towel to your toothbrush bristles and other grooming products. A toiletry bag will protect these items in addition to providing an alternative surface for resting your grooming gear on while at the sink. Regardless of what you do at home, realize that setting toothbrushes and razors on locker room sinks is *not* a great idea.

Wash right. If you don't intend to shower at the gym, wash your hands before heading out. The build-up of bacteria and germs is common on workout equipment and machinery – especially during cold season.

THE GROOMING ISSUE:
THE TWO-MINUTE SAFETY CHECK

THE FACTS:

Most SharpMen would be surprised to learn what details they *fail* to notice before running out the door. Of course, these are the very details that *are* noticed (and snickered at) by your boss, co-workers and the ladies you were hoping to impress. Oops.

THE GROOMING SOLUTION:

The next time you head out the door, take two minutes for this no-brainer safety check:

Step One: Head. Starting at the top, check your hair; it is neat? If possible, keep your hair trimmed, including the stuff on the back of your neck that makes you look like a primate between trips to the barber. See the *Making Your Haircut Last* section of this guidebook for more information.

Check your eyes: is there gunk in the corners? Wash your glasses; spots on the lenses can be distracting to people talking to you.

Look up your nostrils; not the greatest view, but it's better for you to check then for someone *else* see it, not tell you about it and let you walk around with it all day (or at least until it falls off onto your shirt).

Ears: get out the cotton swabs. Gently clean the outer canal. Resist the urge to jam the swab into your ear and mess up your eardrums. See the *Ear Care* section of this guidebook for more information.

Cheeks and chin: any shaving nicks or food crumbs?

Step Two: Body. Did you remember to use deodorant? Take a quick look at the back of your shirt; is your collar tucked in? How about the rest of your clothing – on a scale of one to ten, how clean or wrinkle-free does it look? Got a pet? Could you use a quick sweep with a lint brush?

Step Three: Feet. Take a quick look at your shoes; could they use a quick towel dusting? How about your shoe laces — are they torn or ratty? Could they use a replacement?

Try the Two-Minute Safety Check. A quick sweep before dates, work and even before trips back home can go a long way towards maintaining your sharp look. You'll be surprised by what you haven't seen before.

INDEX

ABOUT THE AUTHORS

THE EDITORS OF SHARPMAN.COM bring you
SHARPMAN.COM, the award-winning men's online community
providing men with "how-to" information on work, dating, grooming,
health and travel. Other books in THE SHARPMAN EDGE series
include:

50 Great Dates for Any Budget

The Young SharpMan's Guide to Grooming:
A How-To Book for SharpMen Ages 13 & Up

How to Make a Pregnant Woman Happy:
Quick & Effective Home Remedies for Over 60 of
Pregnancies Most Common Problems

For more information on SharpMan Press books and other
products, visit www.sharpman.com or contact SharpMan Press at:

SharpMan Press
11718 Barrington Court, No. 702
Los Angeles, CA 90049-2930
866-SHARPMAN (866-742-7762)
orders@sharpman.com